A COMMENTARY ON THE
KĀLACAKRA TANTRA

Taught by
Geshe Lharampa Ngawang Dhargyey

Translated by
Gelong Jhampa Kelsang (Allan Wallace)

Coordinating Editor: Ivanka Vana Jakić

Presented at

Sakya Tegchen Choling
Seattle, Washington, U.S.A.

April 3 – June 12, 1982

LIBRARY OF TIBETAN WORKS & ARCHIVES

Published by the Library of Tibetan Works & Archives, Dharmsala, Himachal Pradesh and Printed by Indraprastha Press (CBT). New Delhi, India.

PUBLISHER'S NOTE

Kālacakra belongs to the class of Highest Yoga Tantra and was originally given by Shakyamuni Buddha to the Dharma King of Shambhala, Suchandra. The lineage was maintained in Shambhala and later passed back to India and then to Tibet where it has been preserved until the present day. Recently the Kālacakra initiation has also been given not only to people from the West, but actually in the Western World. However, authentic publications concerning Kālacakra in English or any other Western language remain extremely rare, so we are particularly happy to be able to publish the present work.

In 1983 LTWA's resident teacher, Geshe Ngawang Dhargyey was invited by some of his long-standing students in Seattle USA to give an explanation of the practice of Kālacakra. The present work is an edited translation of that teaching and contains advice concerning the various commitments and initial practices peculiar to the Kālacakra system within the context of Highest Yoga Tantra in general.

The oral teaching was first translated from Tibetan into English by Gelong Jampa Kelsang (Alan Wallace) and the subsequent transcript was meticulously edited and prepared for publication under the able supervision of Ivanka Vana Jakić. The completed copy was then offered to Geshe Ngawang Dhargyey for review.

We are most grateful to all who have contributed their efforts to this project, particularly to the teacher, translator and editor, and also to Venerable Dagchen Sakya Rinpoche and Dagmo Kusho who kindly offered a location for the teaching in their centre Sakya Tegchen Choling.

Sale and distribution of this book is restricted. We urgently request that only initiates into Highest Yoga Tantra and preferably into the Kālacakra system itself should read it. This caution is customary to the tradition, but to disregard it can only be detrimental. That said we hope that the work will be of benefit to those serious students interested in practising this impeccable path to Buddhahood for the welfare of living beings.

Gyatso Tshering
DIRECTOR

Those who have received the Kālacakra initiation can obtain copies upon request from:

Sakya Tegchen Choling
5042 18th Avenue N.E.
Seattle, Washington 98105
U.S.A.

Naropa Institute Bookstore
2011 – 10th Street
Boulder, Colorado 80302
U.S.A.

Tharpa Choeling
Centre des Hautes Etudes Tibétaines
1801 Mont-Pèlerin
Switzerland,
Europe

RIGPA
Tibetan Buddhist Meditation and Study Centre
44 St. Paul's Crescent
London NW1 9TN
England,
Europe

Library of Tibetan Works and Archives
Gangchen Kyishong
Dharamsala – 176215
Himachal Pradesh,
India

PREFACE

The peerless supreme guide of all gods and living beings, his name in reality being the Omniscient Protector, is His Holiness Tenzin Gyatso Pal Zangpo. The mere hearing of his name provides protection from the fears of existence and quiescence.

As a result of his kindness, I who am his devoted disciple, Geshe Ngawang Dhargyey, have received the complete initiation of Śri-Kalācakra, the King of Tantras, together with the scriptural reading and instructions.

In 1982, at Sakya Tegchen Choling, in Seattle, Washington, U.S.A., I gave a series of teachings based on the Profound Instructions of Śri-Kalācakra, composed by Gyeltsab Chöje, which is like an eye with which to perceive the meaning of the Tantra, and is unlike other traditions of explication of the King of Tantras.

I hope that the transcript of those explanations, which has been prepared in book-form with altruistic intentions by Ivanka Vana Jakić, and with which I am also pleased, will be of great benefit to many fortunate students.

May all sentient beings, our own aged mothers filling all of space, quickly achieve the supreme attainment of Mahāmudrā, the state of empty form.

Geshe Lharampa, Ngawang Dhargyey

Library of Tibetan Works and Archives
Dharamsala, India
April 4, 1983

FOREWORD

Between July 1981 and October 1982, for the first time on the North American continent, approximately 3,000 people received the Kālacakra initiation from His Holiness Tenzin Gyatso, the Fourteenth Dalai Lama, in Madison, Wisconsin, and from the Venerable Kalu Rinpoche, in New York and San Francisco. Through this act of generosity especially extraordinary because it has manifested at a time when the possibility of a nuclear war threatens all life on our planet with extinction, the masters have bestowed upon initiates the timeless legacy of method and wisdom by which Ultimate Goodness can be attained.

For reasons apparent and unknown, the Kalācakra tradition is making its way to the West. With this awareness and with the motivation to benefit those who have received the initiation, I requested the basic teachings on the Kalācakra Tantra from His Holiness and the Venerable Geshe Lharampa Ngawang Dhargyey. With the encouragement of His Holiness, Geshe Dhargyey graciously consented to give a series of lectures on the subject in the Spring of 1982, while he was in Seattle as a Visiting Professor at the University of Washington. We were fortunate that Gelong Jhampa Kelsang (Alan Wallace) accepted the difficult task of acting as interpreter, and that the ideal environment of the Sakya Tegchen Choling was made available through the kindness of its founders, the Venerable Jigdal Dagchen Sakya Rinpoche and Dagmo Kusho.

The twelve teaching sessions offered between April 3 and June 12, 1982 were transcribed from thirteen ninety-minute tapes. Long before the initial typing was completed, it was decided that the material should not be presented simply as rough unauthorized class notes. To make absolutely certain that no omissions or misinterpretations occurred, all tapes had been transcribed twice before a copy was sent to Gelong Jhampa Kelsang for approval. During a subsequent discussion, both of us agreed that the teachings would be presented as a practical manual, the implementation of which presupposed some reorganization of the word-for-word transcript, and that I would be responsible for outlining and organizing the material.

Since Geshe Dhargyey did not only follow Gyeltsab Je's commentary on the Kalācakra Tantra but also drew from the vast treasury of oral transmissions received from his own masters, there was some initial difficulty in organizing the material. However, most of the titles that appear within the major headings of the present manual were given by the Venerable Geshe himself, and the outline that has finally emerged seems to have done so naturally and of it own accord.

Because the teachings represent a vast exposition on a complex subject, they have been arranged into a more manageable and sequential form to make them readily accessible from the standpoint of actual practice. Due to this consideration of changes in organization, the twelve original teaching sessions have been consolidated into ten sections. Once this rough outline was conceived, I made a journey to Vajrapani Institute (Boulder Creek, California) to consult with the Venerable Geshe about the proposed changes. His full approval and encouragement have been the source of inspiration and have provided the energy necessary to carry this idea through to its completion.

Geshe Dhargyey's exposition flows readily from one teaching session to the next and it has been organized according to the format given in the Table of Contents. To facilitate a better overall understanding, material has been shifted, in some cases, from one section to another. An example of such reorganization is found in the instructions on vows and pledges. In the second week of the course, Geshe Dhargyey taught the fourteen root tantric downfalls in accordance with the Kalācakra system and the twenty-five modes of behaviour. Later, during the latter part of the tenth and the entire eleventh session, he gave extensive commentary on the fourteen general root tantric downfalls, the eight secondary tantric downfalls, the commitments of the nineteen pledges, and so forth. All of these teachings have been brought under one heading and can be found in Sections Two and Three.

The most important change has been made by shifting the

practical instructions on the vajra recitation and the vase-like meditation. They were originally taught in the seventh session as a part of the explanation on the ten energies, the four drops, and the importance of guru devotion. However, from the functional point of view, and in this particular context, the two meditational practices represent an integral part of the exposition on the third branch of the practice on the stage of completion called 'life-effort.'* For this reason, the reader will find them in Section Nine of this volume.

Since the presentation was oral, a great deal of wordiness, naturally prevalent in spoken language, was conscientiously edited by Richard Baldwin and Bill Johnson who took special care to preserve the original atmosphere of the teaching situation without obstructing the natural flow of the written language. For this reason alone, the current volume is slightly smaller than the original transcripts. However, I would like to emphasize that nothing presented in the teachings has been either excluded or changed. Notwithstanding any apparent modal inadequacies, the teachings preserved shall always be priceless and unaffected by the current instrument of organization.

Equivalents in Sanskrit and/or Tibetan have been provided whenever available and appropriate. Square brackets are employed for my own interpolations. I have also included a number of cross references in the hope that the reader may more readily see and appreciate the inter-relatedness of all sections, and thus arrive at a more comprehensive understanding of the entire text. Furthermore, because of the complex subject presented in such a relatively short time, a few basic annotations have been provided with the hope that they may be helpful to the majority of Dharma students and practitioners who might be unaware of the availability of the related literature already translated into English. Due to restrictions of time, I was barely able to discover or refer to recent translations of works dealing with the subject of tantra in general, and with Kalācakra Tantra in particular. It is my sincere hope that

*This same sequence of material also appears in the notes to the Kālacakra, "To Entice the Minds of the Wise," written by Gyalwa Gedun Drup, the First Dalai Lama, was stated by Glenn H. Mullin in "Bridging the Sutras and Tantras" (Ithaca: Gabriel Press, 1982), pp. 147–8.

the reader will befriend the reference works cited and will use them as invaluable supplements to this commentary. It cannot be stressed enough that this volume is only an initial attempt to explore the inconceivably rich tradition of one of the most profound subjects of tantra. It would be very important for even a moderately serious student, let alone a practitioner, to clarify areas that have remained unresolved and to answer questions that naturally arise as a result of in-depth reading, by conducting a comparative study of the available authoritative sources and by working closely with a qualified teacher.

I would like to express my most profound indebtedness to His Holiness the Dalai Lama for transforming a dream into reality and for graciously fulfilling a wish of a relatively large number of Western disciples who, otherwise, might not have had the opportunity to receive these invaluable teachings directly through the unbroken oral transmission. I am equally indebted to the Venerable Geshe Ngawang Dhargyey for skillfully and compassionately instructing us in methods by which we will, eventually, be able to comprehend the true nature of the dream-like quality of that same reality.

My very special thanks go to Gelong Jhampa Kelsang whose excellent interpreting made it possible for us to begin the process of bringing up to the conscious level some of the intuitive guesses and the often undefined questions about tantra, as well as the possibility of assimilating some of its aspects into our everyday lives.

I wish to acknowledge my heartfelt gratitude to the Venerable Jigdal Dagchen Sakya Rinpoche, the Founder and Spiritual Director of the Sakya Tegchen Choling, Dagmo Kusho and the members of their center for their kind support and warm hospitality.

For their time, guidance and helpful suggestions concerning the original sources of reference, I would also like to express my deep appreciation to T. G. Dhonthog Rinpoche, Thepo Tulku Rinpoche, Geshe Lobsang Gyatso, Geshe Thubten Gedun, Professor Jeffrey Hopkins, and Professor David S. Ruegg.

A tremendous amount of effort has been expended in the production of this volume by a great number of friends. The process of transmutation from tapes to the completed book had many different aspects and even a greater number of difficulties. Grateful acknowledgement is expressed to the following people: Christina Clark, Elizabeth Heath, Ken Hockett, Bill Johnson, Bill Lerner, Lorraine Lester, Betty McGowan and Carl Yoder for investing long hours in providing a word-for-word transcription of the tapes; Christina Clark, Elizabeth Heath, Judith Lundberg and Debbie Roland for the initial typing; Richard Baldwin and Bill Jonson for their endless hours spent on editing, discussing, and polishing the final version of the text. All of us are indebted to Judith-Ann Robertson for her painstaking typing of the original manuscript. We express our heartfelt gratitude to Diana Reed, Judith-Ann Robertson and Tsering Yuthok for their patience and perseverance in producing the final copy. Their contribution is indeed greatly appreciated. Special thanks go to Peter Allen, Elizabeth Heath and Debbie Roland for proofreading the material.

We are greatly indebted to the anonymous sponsor who kindly donated the initial funds necessary for Geshe Dhargyey's visit to the West and to our dear friends Roderick and Violet Cassidy for their exceptional generosity in unquestioningly and selflessly sponsoring these teachings. Without their aid and constant moral support, even the best of our intentions could not have materialized.

This volume is a labour of love dedicated, with the highest motivation of benefiting all that lives to the long lives of His Holiness the Dalai Lama and all our precious teachers of the Three Vehicles. Furthermore, it is offered as a small contribution to the gigantic task of transplanting the Dharma to the West, with the hope that deeper appreciation of our ultimate goal as Mahāyāna-Dharma students and practitioners may be born. May whatever merit acquired collectively and individually, by preserving the pure unbroken oral transmission from the East to the West, nurture greater understanding and peace among all people in the world.

Ivanka Vana Jakić

Seattle, Washington
July 1982 – November 1983

xi

CONTENTS

MAÑJUŚRĪ*

Obeisance to my Guru and Protector, Mañjuśrī,
   Who holds to his heart a scriptural text
      symbolic of his seeing all things as they are,
   Whose intelligence shines forth as the sun,
      unclouded by delusions or traces of ignorance
   Who teaches in sixty ways, with the loving compassion
      of a father for his only son,
         all creatures caught in the prison of saṃsāra,
      confused in the darkness of their ignorance,
      overwhelmed by their suffering.
You, whose dragon-thunder-like proclamation of Dharma
      arouses us from the stupor of our delusions
      and frees us from the iron chains of our karma.
   Who wields the sword of wisdom hewing down suffering
      wherever its sprouts appear,
      clearing away the darkness of ignorance.
You, whose princely body is adorned with the one hundred
      and twelve marks of a Buddha,
   Who has completed the stages achieving
      the highest perfection of a Bodhisattva,
   Who has been pure from the beginning,
I bow down to you, O Mañjuśrī,
With the brilliance of your wisdom, O compassionate one,
Illuminate the darkness enclosing my mind.
Enlighten my intelligence and wisdom
      so that I may gain insight
Into Buddha's words and the texts that explain them.

*Daily Recitations of Preliminaries, 4th Ed. (Dharamsala: Library of Tibetan Works and Archives, 1975), p. 9.

MAÑJUŚRĪ

la.ma d'ang gönpo je.tzün jam.päl.yang.la ch'ag.tsäl.lo.

g'ang.g'i lo.dr'ö drib.nyi trin.dr'äl nyi.tar namd'ag rab.säl.wä.

j'i.nye d'ön.kün j'i.zhin zig.ch'ir nyi.kyi t'ug.kar leg.b'am.dzin.

g'ang.d'ag si.pai tzön.rar ma.rig mun.t'om dug.ngäl gy'i.zer.wä.

dro.tsog kün.la b'u. chig tar.tze yän.lag dr'ug.chui yang.dän.sung.

drug.tar ch'er.drog nyön.mong nyi.long lä.kyi chag.drog dröl.d-
zä.ching.

ma.rig mün.sel dug.ngäl nyu.g'u j'i.nye chö.dze ral.dr'i.nam.

dö.nä d'ag.ching sa.chui t'ar.sön yön.tän lü.dzog gyäl.sä t'u.wö-
.ku.

chu.tr'ag chu.d'ang chu.nyi gyän.trä dag.lo mün.sel jam.päl.yang-
.la.dü.

tze.dän ky'o.kyi ky'en.rab wö.zer.g'yi dag.loi ti.mug mün.pa
rab.säl.nä.

ka.d'ang tän.cho zhung.lug tog.pay.yi.

lo.dr'ö pob.pai nang.wa tzäl.d'u.söl.

SECTION ONE

It is of very great importance to cultivate a proper motivation for receiving these teachings. Not just any motivation will do. Since the Kālacakra Tantra is a means of attaining full enlightenment of Buddhahood within one short lifetime, the motivation to be cultivated is to listen to the teachings with the intent of reaching enlightenment ever so swiftly for the great benefit of all sentient beings. Rather than listening to the teachings as mere words, check your own mind and actually cultivate this motivation.

As we receive these teachings we should imagine ourselves not simply being in an ordinary house made of brick and mortar, but rather generate ourselves inside the palace of Kālacakra, that is, a splendid palace of jewels and of light. Likewise, with regard to the Master who is giving the teachings, we should cast aside ordinary appearance. In fact, in the stage of generation on the path of tantra the chief points of refutation are the ordinary appearance and ordinary grasping (ordinary conceptualization). Applying this to the present situation, abandon the ordinary appearance of the Teacher and generate him, or look upon him, as the natural manifestation of Kālacakra. In the same way, those of us who are receiving the teachings should also abandon our ordinary appearance and concept of our own selves and generate ourselves in the simple form of Kālacakra with two hands and fully adorned with the ornaments.

I. THE MEANS FOR PROGRESSING ALONG THE PATH OF KĀLACAKRA

A. THE MEANS FOR BECOMING A SUITABLE VESSEL

TRAINING IN THE COMMON PATH

In the progression of the practice, first of all there is the motivation, the attitude. In the words of the great master, Dragpa

3

Gyeltsen, "If one clings to this life, one is not a spiritual person."[1] One should draw one's clinging away from the affairs of this life and look rather to the life beyond.

Secondly, from the same master, "If one grasps at the bounties and pleasures of the cycle of existence, including those of humans and gods, there is no renunciation, the emergent mind." It is important to recognize that whatever pleasures or bounties arise in the entire cycle of existence are without essence and they are by [their] nature unstable. One needs to turn one's mind away from pleasures and fortunes and, in this way, generate renunciation.

Thirdly, "If one clings to personal well-being there is no awakening mind (Skt. bodhicitta; Tib. byang. chub. kyi. sems)." The point here is that one must turn the mind away from concern for one's own welfare to that of others. This is something that should really be put into practice.

Fourthly, "If there occurs grasping, there is not the view (Skt.dṛṣti; Tib. lta. ba)" 'Grasping' here refers to the conceptualization of true existence. Although we conceive of things as existing inherently since they do appear [to us] or seem to exist from their own side, in fact, there is no such thing as true existence. Phenomena do not really exist in this way (from their own side inherently), but rather as mere conceptual imputations. As long as one is still conceiving of phenomena as being truly existent, one does not have the 'view,' that is, the realistic view, the view of the middle way.

These verses summarize what is called the common training. It is called 'common' because it exists in both the sūtra and the tantra paths. Within these verses are presented the emergent mind or renunciation, the awakening mind of bodhicitta, and the realistic view. These three are what is necessary in order to fully enter the tantric path. If they are missing the tantric path does not bear fruit. Particularly, the awakening mind is essential. If it is lacking, no matter how much one practices tantra it will not lead to full enlightenment; it will not even lead to the Mahāyāna path of accumulation which is the first of the five Mahāyāna paths.

There are two paths for attaining full enlightenment: the causal path of the Sūtrayāna and the resultant path of the Vajrayāna. Of these two, Vajrayāna is superior. Among the great paṇḍitas of ancient India, the very profound path of tantra was as renowned as the sun and the moon.

Within the Vajrayāna there are four general tantric paths:
1. The Action Tantra (Skt. kriyā-tantra; Tib. bya. rgyud).
2. The Performance Tantra (Skt. caryā-tantra; Tib. spyod. rgyud).
3. Yoga Tantra (Skt. yoga-tantra; Tib. rnal. 'byor. rgyud).
4. The Highest Yoga or Supreme Yoga Tantra (Skt. annuttara yoga-tantra; Tib. rnal. 'byor. bla. med).

Among these four, the Supreme Yoga Tantra is extremely profound. It provides the means to attain full enlightenment with one body in one lifetime.

In the Supreme Yoga Tantra, there are the male tantras and the female tantras. The Kālacakra Tantra is a female tantra. What is the general distinction between the male and female tantras? The female tantras particularly emphasize wisdom, that is, the emptiness aspect. Translating into tantric terms, this refers to the 'clear light.' The male tantras emphasize the method aspect, which refers specifically to the 'illusory body.'

Individuals who have not yet entered the path toward enlightenment, and those who are fundamentally capable of attaining full enlightenment in one life with one body, must be born from a womb and be endowed with six factors (Tib. khams. drug). In essence, this means that one must be a human being of this realm (Skt. jambudvīpa). There are different ways of describing the six factors. According to one, the blood, flesh and skin are received from the mother, and the bones, marrow and white bodhicitta from the father. Another presentation is that of the four elements (earth, water, fire and air), plus the channels of energy (Skt. nādī; Tib. rtsa) and the 'drops' (Skt. bindu; Tib. thig. le).

A lot of information is being given here and we hear a lot of words. But it is insufficient to simply leave it at that and say, "Here, now I have this information." The point is that this teaching should be meditated upon. One needs to engage in the practice not only for some days, but for weeks and months. The mind is gradually transformed in this way. Likewise, the emergent mind (renunciation), the awakening mind (bodhicitta), and the realistic view (the view of the middle way) should be cultivated.

We have minds which are fit for the cultivation of all of them. They, as well as our own minds, are impermanent phenomena. Given the proper causes and conditions, these three aspects can arise in one's own continuum. So, it is very important to put these teachings into practice. The people who are receiving these instructions are not simply here to gather some intellectual knowledge but, having received the empowerment, have come here to receive the teachings in order to put them into practice. It is very important that we really apply what we hear.

There are two very different ways of receiving the teachings. One is the worldly way, simply gathering information to gain greater knowledge and also greater reputation and position, and so forth. In tantra, this type of attitude or motivation is totally unsuitable. The point here is to receive the teachings in order to transform one's own mental continuum.

In order to practice the Kālacakra, first of all, it is absolutely essential to receive the empowerment. Furthermore, the master from whom one receives the empowerment should be a fully qualified tantric master who bears the 20 qualities signifying such a master. These 20 include ten outer qualities and ten inner qualities. Furthermore, for the empowerment one needs to have a completely accurate mandala made exactly the right way.[2] What is required of the practitioners? The disciples must be well trained in the common path (which has already been presented), and have both a very firm faith and enthusiasm for tantra.

B. RIPENING ONE'S MIND BY MEANS OF THE EMPOWERMENT

For the Kālacakra there are seven empowerments which are like a child growing up. These seven are called 'Empowerments of Entering Like a Child.' One needs to receive all of the seven empowerments [in order to be able and allowed] to meditate on the stage of generation.

THE SEVEN EMPOWERMENTS OF ENTERING 'LIKE A CHILD'

1. The First Empowerment – The Water Empowerment

Just as mother having given birth immediately washes the child with water, in like fashion, the master first gives the water empowerment for cleansing the three doors, that is, the body, speech and mind of the initiates.

2. The Second Empowerment – The Empowerment of the Headdress

The analogy here is that the hair on the child's head is simply left. This empowerment acts as a cause for the eventual attainment of the uṣṇīṣa (the crown protrusion of a Buddha) when oneself becomes a Buddha. It is very fortunate to be able to receive such an empowerment.

3. The Third Empowerment – The Empowerment of the Crown Banner

This represents the five Buddha Families and is likened to putting ornaments on the child, such as earrings.

4. The Fourth Empowerment – The Empowerment of the Vajra and Bell

Of special importance in this analogy is the bell which corresponds to the child laughing. The vajra and bell in this empowerment are especially related to the Buddha-Mind and the Buddha-Speech. Receiving this empowerment places imprints upon one's own continuum for giving such a result.

5. The Fifth Empowerment – The Empowerment of the Thumb-Vajra

This is analogous to putting an ornament on the child's thumb.

6. The Sixth Empowerment – The Empowerment of the Name

This is analogous to naming the infant.

7. The Seventh Empowerment – Initiation

The Tibetan word for this empowerment is 'je. nang' (rjes.g-nang), which translates as 'initiation' or 'permission.' This is analogous to the father or the mother teaching the child.

The essential significance is that by receiving the seven empowerments, one is empowered to practice the stage of generation. The first seven empowerments of 'entering like a child' also empower or cause one to gain the first seven Bodhisattva grounds as follow:

a. The water empowerment leads and gives rise to the first ground, the Very Joyful (Skt. pramuditā; Tib. rab.tu.dga-'.ba).

b. The headdress empowerment gives rise to the second ground, the Stainless (Skt. vimalā; Tib. dri.ma.med.pa).

c. The crown banner empowerment gives rise to the third ground, the Luminous (Skt. prabhākarī; Tib. 'od.byed.pa).

d. The vajra and bell empowerment gives rise to the fourth ground, the Radiant (Skt. arcismatī; Tib. 'od. 'phro.ba).

e. The thumb-vajra empowerment gives rise to the fifth ground, Difficult to Conquer (Skt. sudurjayā; Tib. sbyang.dka'.ba).

f. The name empowerment gives rise to the sixth ground, the Manifesting One (Skt. abhimukhī; Tib. mngon.du.gyur.ba).

g. The empowerment of permission or initiation gives rise to the seventh ground, the Far Gone One (Skt. dūramgamā; Tib. ring.du.song.ba).

THE FOUR HIGHER EMPOWERMENTS

1. The First Empowerment – The Empowerment of the Vase

The point of this empowerment is to ripen the mind of the trainee. First, one imagines offering a girl, between the ages of 12 and 20, to the vajra master. Together with this, one offers the mandala and prayers to the vajra master and requests the empowerment.

The vase empowerment is actually given when the imagined girl comes back to the trainee who then enjoys her presence through laughing and fondling her breasts. As one touches the girl's breasts there arises the 'bliss' (Skt. sukha; Tib. bde.ba) which should be experienced as indivisible from emptiness. It is with this experience of indivisible emptiness and bliss that one actually receives the vase empowerment. There is not actually any vase or any pot that is used for this empowerment. What is referred to as 'the pot' are the breasts of the girl, which are called the 'vase that holds the white'[3] (Tib. dkar. 'dzin.gyi.bum.pa). Because one touches the breasts of the girl and the breasts are likened to the vase, this is called the empowerment of the vase.

8

The vase empowerment leads one to the attainment of the eighth Bodhisattva ground called the Immovable (Skt. acalā; Tib. mi.g.yo.ba).

The ninth Bodhisattva ground is called the Good Intelligence (Skt. sādhumatī; Tib. legs.pa'i.blo.gros). The tenth Bodhisattva ground, called the Cloud of Dharma (Skt. dharma-meghā; Tib. chos. kyi.sprin), is the highest of the Bodhisattva grounds. There is no place to go from there except Buddhahood. By the time you get there you are in a very fine place indeed.

2. The Second Empowerment – The Secret Empowerment

The second of these four higher empowerments is the secret empowerment. During the empowerment, one imagines that the secret vajra of the vajra master is placed in the mouth of the trainee and one tastes the white bodhicitta of the vajra master. This white bodhicitta goes down to the heart-cakra of the devotee and there arises 'great bliss' (Tib.bde.chen.po). This bliss is experienced with the realization of emptiness, which is essential. With this unified experience of bliss and emptiness one receives the secret empowerment.

It should be re-emphasized that, because of the nature of the empowerment and the nature of the practice, it is absolutely vital for trainees to have full faith in the tantra. This is called the secret empowerment because the secret substance of the vajra master is experienced.

3. The Third Empowerment – The Wisdom Empowerment

The third of the higher empowerments is called the wisdom empowerment. It is received in the following way: a visualized consort, or ḍākinī-consort, is given to the trainee and they enter sexual union. From this union the white bodhicitta descends from the crown of one's head. When it arrives at the throat-cakra there arises 'joy' (Skt. ānanda; Tib.dga'.ba). When it descends to the heart-cakra there arises 'supreme joy' (Skt. parama-ānanda; Tib. mchog.dga'). When it descends to the navel-cakra there arises 'extraordinary joy' (Skt. virama-ānanda; Tib. khyad.par.gyi.dga-'.ba). And when it descends to the genital-cakra there arises the 'spontaneous joy' (Tib. lhan.skyes.kyi.dga'.ba), which is the highest of these four. One experiences this fourth type of Joy while ascertaining its empty nature. With that unified experience of both the bliss and the realization of emptiness, one receives the wisdom empowerment. It is so called because the ḍākinī, the consort herself, being of the nature of wisdom is called prajñā or wisdom. When one speaks of the white and red bodhicitta it should be pointed out that it is not only males that have the white bodhicitta, or only females who have the red – both sexes have both. It is simply a matter of dominance. Even while receiving this empowerment where one goes into union with a consort, if one is a woman, one is still generating oneself in the form of Kālacakra and is receiving the initiation in that state. There is no contradiction in that sense. Likewise, to take just another example of Vajrayoginī (Tib. rdo.rje.rnal.'byor.ma), if one is a man, one receives this empowerment and engages in the practice while generating oneself in the feminine aspect of Vajrayoginī.

4. The Fourth Empowerment – The Empowerment of the Word

Without allowing the white bodhicitta to come out, but retaining it, one experiences the 'supreme immutable bliss' (Tib. mchog.tu-.mi. 'gyur.ba' i.bde.ba). With the experience of this bliss one receives the word empowerment. To allow the white bodhicitta to come out is actually a root downfall in this tantra. It is something to be absolutely avoided.

THE FOUR HIGHER HIGHER EMPOWERMENTS

Finally, there are four higher, higher empowerments. These have the same names as the preceding four in the same order: the vase, the secret, the wisdom and the word. The distinction between the four higher and the four higher, higher empowerments is in what is actually occurring.

One distinction between the two is that the higher empowerments are given in terms of the conventional truth (Skt. samvrtisatya; Tib. kun.rdzob.bden.pa). The four higher, higher empowerments are given in terms of the actual meaning (Tib. nges.don) and the supramundane (Tib. 'jig.rten.las.das.pa), that is, the actual supramundane aspect or approach.

The four higher, higher empowerments are the ultimate

empowerments in this cycle. These four higher, higher empowerments empower or allow one to perform the activities of the vajrācārya or vajra master, involving both giving empowerment as well as explaining the tantra.

1. The First Empowerment – The Vase Empowerment

During the vase empowerment, the white bodhicitta descends from the crown-cakra to the point between the eyebrows (Tib. smin.mtshams) in the central channel and one experiences 'joy' (Skt. ānanda; Tib. dga'.ba). It is with the experience of this joy that one actually receives the vase initiation.

2. The Second Empowerment – The Secret Empowerment

The secret empowerment is the empowerment in which the trainee goes into union with the consort or dākinī. When the white bodhicitta descends [from the point between the eyebrows] down to the heart-cakra, one experiences the 'supreme joy' (Skt. parama-ānanda; Tib. mchog.dga'). That experience is the receiving of the secret empowerment.

3. The Third Empowerment – The Wisdom Empowerment

During the empowerment of wisdom, with the trainee and consort in union, the white bodhicitta descends [from the heart-cakra] to the genital-cakra at which point one experiences the 'special' or 'extraordinary joy' (Skt. virama-ānanda; Tib. khyad.dga').

The actual receiving of the empowerment of wisdom occurs with the experience of 'spontaneous joy' (Skt. sahaja-ānanda; Tib. lhan.skyes.kyi.dga'.ba) when the white bodhicitta reaches the very tip of the genital organ. For very highly realized beings, the white bodhicitta is not ejected at all but is retained by the force of the 'wind' or 'energy' (Skt. prāna; Tib. rlung).

4. The Fourth Empowerment – The Empowerment of the Word

The gradual cultivation of the stage of generation (Skt. utpatti-krama; Tib. bskyed.rim) and completion (Skt. sampanna-krama; Tib. rdzogs.rim), which are developed by repeatedly engaging in the practice of meditation, eventually culminates in the actual state of full enlightenment. At that point one achieves

11

the Body (Tib. rlung.sems) of Kālacakra. This is not an ordinary, gross body made of flesh and bones like our present body, but is created simply from energy (Tib. rlung) and consciousness (Tib. sems). This is the culmination of the tantric path.

The empowerment of the word is received when one gains an understanding that this is how the tantric path culminates. In other words, one understands that the culmination of the tantric path is [of] the nature of the 'great union' (Tib. zung.' jug).

It is pointed out that if one is a monk (Skt. bhiksu; Tib; dge.slong) or a lay practitioner with vows of celibacy then, in receiving these empowerments, one does not have an actual consort and does not receive the empowerments in the way just described. Not only a fully ordained monk, but anyone who has the vows of going forth (Tib. rab.'byung.sdom.pa), which include the vow of celibacy, will not receive this empowerment with an actual consort. In such a case, the trainee visualizes both the consort and the entire process during the initiation. Furthermore, the empowerment utilizing an actual consort is not given to elderly people who no longer have the red and white bodhicitta but rather by means of visualization. However, if one is very highly realized, then it is possible to take the empowerment with the consort as has just been described. But, one needs to be very highly realized and not just an ordinary monk. This indicates that there are two types of consort:

'Action Mudrā' (Skt. karma-mudrā; Tib. las.kyi.phyag.rgya). An action mudrā is an actual consort, a real person. It is stressed once again that it is not with this type of consort that an ordinary monk receives such an empowerment.

'Wisdom Mudrā' (skt. jñāna-mudrā; Tib. ye.shes.kyi.phyag. rgya). This is a visualized consort. It is with this latter type that an ordinary monk or other persons with vows of celibacy would receive this empowerment.

THE FOUR TYPES OF JOY AS RELATED TO THE FOUR BODIES OF A BUDDHA

These four types of joy, one by one, correspondingly give rise to the four Bodies (Skt. kāya; Tib. sku) of a Buddha.

1. The first, called joy (Skt. ānanda; Tib. dga'ba), leads to the attainment of the Emanation Body (Skt. nirmānakāya; Tib. sprul.sku).

2. The second, supreme joy (Skt. parama-ānanda; Tib. mchog.dga') leads to the attainment of the Enjoyment Body (Skt. sambhogakāya; Tib. longs.sku).

3. The third, extraordinary joy (Skt. virama-ānanda; Tib. khyad.dga'), gives rise to the Wisdom Truth Body of the Buddha (Skt. jñāna-dharma-kāya; Tib. ye.shes.chos.sku).

4. The fourth, spontaneous joy (Skt. sahaja-ānanda; Tib. lhan.skyes.kyi.dga'ba), gives rise to the Nature Truth Body of the Buddha (Skt. svabhāvika-kāya; Tib. ngo.bo.nyid.sku).

A verse from Milarepa praises his guru, Marpa the Great, in the following way, "I prostrate at Marpa's feet who has arisen from the great lineage of tantra (mantra) and who embodies the four types of joy."

Upon receiving this empowerment, it is indispensible to keep the pledges and the vows. Quoting a scripture, "Even if one does not engage in the meditation of tantra but keeps the pledges and the vows without the occurrence of a root downfall, one certainly attains full enlightenment within 16 lifetimes." The great translator Ralo Dorje Drak said, "If one does not keep the pledges and the precepts of tantra, the Buddha has not stated that one will then attain supreme enlightenment. Not only will one not reach supreme enlightenment, but one will not even attain siddhis (powers or boons) from the practice." The practice is not effective without keeping the pledges and precepts.

In this large city of Seattle there are many, many people. Among them the number who actually go to receive Dharma teachings is very small. Even in a family where the parents take the children to the temple and show them how to make prostrations and offerings, if the child does not have the merit or imprints, it is very difficult and faith may not arise. So, keep the pledges and precepts (as difficult as it may seem) and recognize the good fortune to be able to receive them in the first place. To be able to receive these teachings, one already has a great store of merit. Furthermore, to have faith in the Buddha-Dharma is also indicative of already having a great store of merit from previous lifetimes. If this merit were missing, faith simply would not arise. One should reflect upon one's good fortune in having the opportunity to receive the empowerment and being able to follow this practice.

We should feel encouraged to engage in the practice of the Kālacakra. We do not need to do so in a very complicated or elaborate way. Rather we should generate ourselves in the simple form of Kālacakra, blue in color with one face and two arms. In Kālacakra's right hand is a vajra and in his left a bell. Kālacakra is in union with the consort who holds in her right hand a cleaver and in her left hand a skull-cup.

This is an especially good practice because it simultaneously fulfills two functions. On the one hand, it is a tantric practice leading to the culmination of the tantric stage of generation, on the other, it is also cultivating and leading to the attainment of 'clear stillness.' By practicing in this way it is not necessary to cultivate clear stillness (Skt. Śamatha; Tib. zhi.gnas) as a separate practice. One attains it naturally through the culmination of the stage of generation. You generate yourself as the Kālacakra deity with the consort – not in the space before you, but you are actually generating yourself in that form. At this time, you cultivate the appearance of the deity and the pride of being this deity. What is the rationale behind this? It is not as if simply some mundane deity, like Īśvara, were to think he was a Buddha. If Īśvara goes around thinking he is a Buddha, it does not make him a Buddha. The sense here is that one is taking the Buddha one will become, identifying with and establishing the pride in that Buddha, and cultivating this in the present. When we are told to "have the pride of being a Buddha, the Buddha that you will become, in the form of the Kālacakra," what is being stated is that Kālacakra is, in actual fact, a manifestation of the Buddha.

How does this relate to the origin of the Kālacakra teachings? While the Buddha was on Vulture's Peak teaching the *Pranjñāpāramitā* (the *Perfection of Wisdom*), he was simultaneously emanating himself in a place in the south of India where, in the form of Kālacakra, he was giving the Kālacakra teachings. The illustration at the beginning of the book, *Kalachakra Initiation, Madison 1981*, is of Dawa Zangpo (lit. 'good moon') who was a king of

14

Shambhala. It was he who requested the Buddha to teach Kālacakra and who was the chief patron. The Buddha then manifested as Kālacakra and the teachings were given.

Engaging in the practice of Kālacakra leads to one's own rebirth in Shambhala where the tantras have greatly flourished and are very widespread. By putting these teachings into practice, the path is open for our own full enlightenment. Kangsar Dorje Chang was a very great recent Tibetan lama who was one of the Root-gurus of both the tutors of His Holiness the Dalai Lama, Kyabje Ling Dorje Chang and Kybje Trijang Dorje Chang. It was from him that Kyabje Ling Dorje Chang, the Senior Tutor to His Holiness, received the lineage that we are receiving here. Kangsar Dorje Chang linked Shambhala to Lhasa in that it is an actual place with villages and towns; it is just truly a delightful place. One can attain full enlightenment there.

To reiterate, while practicing the stage of generation, the main objective is to dispel the ordinary appearance and ordinary conceptions (grasping). One way of doing this while looking at any kind of form, even when looking upon a snow mountain, is to see the object (of visual perception) as being the body of Kālacakra. And for any sound that is heard, comprehend this as being the speech of Kālacakra. And whenever thoughts arise in one's own mind, be they good or bad, imagine them to be the mind of Kālacakra. This is something to be practiced all the time, even as you are driving down the freeway. It becomes a very practical way of dispelling ordinary appearances and conceptions.

It is very important to recognize the distinction of the special forms of tantra. What is its distinctiveness? With Cakrasamvara, Guhyasamāja and so forth, it is important to recognize the individual distinguishing factors of these different meditational deities and thereby understand how they differ from ordinary deities like Īśvara. Recognizing in this way the profundity of tantra, there arises faith in it. In the process of practicing tantra one learns the means for dispelling attachment by means of attachment. It is like the insect that is born from wood, comes out of a tree and then turns around and eats the wood of the tree.

15

NOTES

[1] The English rendering of quotations from books and verbal statements from former masters should be considered as paraphrases and not as strict translations.

[2] From the base of the maṇḍala in some other tantras there are successive maṇḍalas of three elements: the wind or energy-maṇḍala, the water-maṇḍala the earth-maṇḍala. The fire-maṇḍala is not explicitly present; its existence is implied because it occurs by the combination of the wind, the water and the earth. In the Kālacakra, on the other hand, from the base of the maṇḍala there are the wind, the fire, the water and the earth maṇḍalas. Thus, the fire is explicitly there. This is one among many distinctions found in this particular tantric system.

[3] 'White' refers to milk in this context.

SECTION TWO

We are encouraged to recognize our great good fortune in having this opportunity to assemble here and receive the Kālacakra teachings. This is a very bountiful and fortunate situation which is really due to the kindness of the Venerable Dagchen Rinpoche. If he had not established this place, we would not be here, and it might have been difficult to find a similar situation. Furthermore, you have frequent contact with Rinpoche which is a very rare event. In Tibet, for example, it was very unlikely, if not impossible, for people to have this direct access to the Sakya Gongma, the high lamas of the Sakya tradition. Therefore, it is important to recognize these rare and precious circumstances.

Westerners may get the idea that it is quite easy to meet such lamas as Dagchen Rinpoche or His Holiness because they do have this access. However, the lamas in Tibet, in terms of personal contact, were far more inaccessible. People would feel with regard to His Holiness the Dalai Lama that if they could just simply have the hand-blessing, the chag wang, on top of the head once a year, this would be a precious event. But nowadays; we can see that in Dharamsala Westerners have frequent contact with His Holiness; they can ask for personal audience and this is often given. Whereas in Tibet, just to be able to gaze upon such a lama would have a tremendous impact.

In addition, you have had the great opportunity of receiving the Kālacakra initiation. It is important to recognize and rejoice in these rare and wonderful events.

II. KEEPING ONE'S VOWS AND PLEDGES

A. THE FOURTEEN ROOT TANTRIC DOWNFALLS

Keeping one's vows and pledges is indispensable if one is to progress along the tantric path. The ones to be especially aware of and to be on guard against are the 14 root tantric downfalls. It is extremely important to avoid a root downfall. Compared to one of the four chief monastic precepts of a fully ordained monk, breaking one of these tantric precepts is an extremely serious infraction. It leaves terrible imprints on the mind with a very heavy karmic result. Even to break a secondary tantric precept (Tib. sbom.po) is more than 18 times heavier than breaking the heaviest of the monastic precepts. To commit one of the root downfalls is an extremely unwholesome and detrimental deed and leads to birth in vajra hell. Therefore, as the *Six-Session Guru Yoga* states, "The 14 root tantric downfalls should be guarded against even at the cost of one's life".

In order to keep the pledges and precepts or in general to keep moral discipline, one needs to recognize and guard the 'four doors' which lead to downfalls. It would be like having a room full of gold with four doors. If one did not guard these four doors, a thief would come in and carry off all the gold. The four doors which lead to the commitment of a downfall are:

1. the door of ignorance,
2. the door of irreverence,
3. the door of carelessness,
4. the door of mental distortion.

If one does not guard these four doors, then every day one will commit downfalls.

In order to guard the first of these four doors, one needs to know what the pledges and precepts are. Going back to the analogy of the room full of gold, to prevent a thief from coming in one needs to be able to recognize who the thieves are.

His Holiness the Dalai Lama, speaking on this subject in Dharamsala, says that it is quite ridiculous how many people go in a carefree way to receive a tantric empowerment and take all of the Bodhisattva precepts, as well as the major and secondary tantric pledges, every one of which is extremely difficult to keep properly; and yet, when it is suggested that they take the vows of monastic ordination, they think, "Oh no, that's much too difficult! I wouldn't even think of that! I'll just take the tantric and Bodhisattva precepts." The Bodhisattva and tantric precepts are actually far more difficult to keep. In comparison, the vows of

18

ordination, which chiefly emphasize the activities of the body and speech, are far easier to keep.

To illustrate this further, one can look to the life of Atīśa. He stated that throughout his whole life he had never incurred the slightest infraction of any of his vows of ordination. On rare occasions he would incur an infraction of one of the Bodhisattva precepts. But he stated that his infractions of the tantric precepts were as common as rain pattering down. If this is true of a highly realized tantric master such as Atīśa, it goes without saying that we are in bad shape.

For example, the breaking of a tertiary tantric precept occurs simply by taking food or drink without blessing it with the three-fold mantra Oṃ Āḥ Hūṃ. Also, failing to bless one's clothes when putting them on is a tertiary fault. This is not a difficult practice. Whenever taking food or drink it is beneficial to bless them with this mantra, Oṃ Āḥ Hūṃ, three times. Likewise, when you put on clothes, bless the clothes. And, for example, when you put on your lower garment, bless it and think of it as a tiger skin.

GENERAL ROOT TANTRIC DOWNFALLS

1. Abusing or having contempt for one's spiritual mentor.

The first of the root precepts involves the relationship with the guru. This downfall occurs through the abuse and contempt for one's spiritual mentor. Once one has brought about a spiritual relationship with the guru, one should relate to this guru properly and have proper devotion towards all of one's spiritual mentors.

2. Contemptuously disregarding the training.

Take a specific precept like the precept of not eating in the afternoon. If one were to say, "Oh, this doesn't matter," and were to toss that precept out very contemptuously and without any respect, one would incur this root downfall.

3. Disparaging or speaking of the faults of a vajra brother or sister.

Be especially cautious of this point. All of us right here and many other of our friends who have received a tantric empowerment from the same guru are vajra brothers and sisters. This relationship is very precious. For example, in an ordinary family, children born of the same parents are said to be siblings. A similar relationship occurs in the tantric practice. In an empowerment there is the process of the devotee entering the mouth of the vajra master, who is generated as Kālacakra, not simply the lama as a person. So, one enters the mouth of Kālacakra and goes into his heart, melts into the bodhicitta with the 'tum.mo flame' (Skt. caṇḍālī; Tib. gtum.mo) at the heart of Kālacakra, descends down to the vajra, and through the vajra of Kālacakra enters the womb of the consort. There one is blessed by the white bodhicitta, the Buddhas and Bodhisattvas. One then emerges from the womb and in this way is truly a spiritual child of Kālacakra (the vajra guru) and the consort. This is true of every individual receiving the empowerment. Recognizing this very special relationship among one's vajra brothers and sisters, one should take special care to avoid disparaging or abusing them or speaking of their faults. Committing this root downfall leads to an unfortunate realm of existence.

In general, it is good never to speak of the faults of anyone. Mahākāśyapa, a great disciple of the Buddha, stated that after the parinirvāṇa of the Buddha, he looked upon all sentient beings as being Buddhas. He said the reason for doing so was because he himself did not know, among the individuals around, whose mind had and whose mind had not been ripened. So, he simply cultivated this general awareness or recognition of sentient beings as being the Buddha.

4. Abandoning loving-kindness (Skt. maitrī; Tib. byams.pa).

This occurs when one looks upon any sentient being thinking, "May this person be separated from happiness." We should be especially cautious with this precept. Although it is unlikely that we would develop a wish that all sentient beings be bereft of happiness, nevertheless, we might very well be inclined to develop such a wish for someone we do not like. In other words, in committing such a downfall it is not necessary to abandon loving-kindness for sentient beings. All that is necessary for such an infraction is to take one individual sentient being, especially a very evil being and, looking upon this person, come to the firm conviction in one's own mind, "Although I might benefit and serve others, I will not benefit and serve this person. Even if I get the opportunity to lead this person to joy, I will not do so." Just abandoning one sentient being constitutes this downfall of abandoning loving-kindness for sentient beings. This indicates the general mood of the Mahāyāna Dharma, in which great compassion is so central, encompassing all sentient beings without exception. So, if one does make an exception, saying, "Yes, generally all sentient beings, but not for this or that person," then there is no longer any great compassion.

We should clearly understand what is meant by loving-kindness (Skt. maitrī; Tib. byams.pa) and compassion (Skt. karuṇā; Tib. snying.rje). The mind wishing that sentient beings may have happiness [and the causes of happiness] is loving-kindness. The mind which wishes to dispel the suffering [and the causes of suffering] of sentient beings is compassion. If one is simply saying, "love and compassion," without understanding the meaning of these two terms, there is not much benefit.

5. Rejecting the yearning-bodhicitta and the engaging-bodhicitta.

Upon receiving the empowerment, one cultivates the aspiration to attain full enlightenment for the benefit of all creatures. One has made this resolution or pledge. Later, if one gets discouraged and loses confidence or enthusiasm for the practice and thinks, "How could I ever do that?" and abandons that aspiration, this root downfall occurs. Therefore, one should always maintain one's courage and confidence in the practice.

Here comes a good story for those of you who are falling asleep. In order to cultivate your courage for the practice, you can look back on the life of Dignāga. Dignāga had been writing a great treatise on one occasion. A non-Buddhist came to debate with him and tried to defeat him and everything he was doing. Dignāga and the non-Buddhist debated, and Dignāga beat him. Seeing that he was defeated, with smoke coming from his nose, the man spit fire from his mouth and burned up Dignāga's robes and all the things around him. Dignāga looked around and saw what had happened and was pretty unhappy. He thought, "In the presence of all the Buddhas and Bodhisattvas, I have made a resolution to attain enlightenment for the benefit of all sentient brings. But if all sentient beings are going to turn out, one by one, like this fellow, it's a losing occupation. How can I ever do this? It seems so impractical." So, he took a stone tablet and tossed it up in the air with the thought, "If this stone tablet falls back to the ground, I'm going to give up bodhicitta, give up that resolution." He threw it up and looked around and did not hear the clunk of the stone falling. He looked up into the sky and there was Mañjuśri holding it up for him. Mañjuśrī told him, "My son, don't do this, don't do this! You must continue! You are very close to falling to the lesser vehicle. You should, by all means, continue writing the text *Pramāṇasamuccaya*. If you do so, it will be unassailable by any non-Buddhist logician and, in the future, it will be like the eyes of wisdom for sentient beings."

This fifth downfall of abandoning the yearning and engaging bodhicittas occurs when one rejects this resolution, thinking, "Ah, how could I ever attain enlightenment for the benefit of all creatures?"

6. Abusing the Dharma – be it of the sūtras or tantras.

This occurs, for example, if out of one's faith in the Mahāyāna, one abuses the Hīnayāna; or out of one's faith in the Hīnayāna, one abuses the Mahāyāna. Also, if one has faith in the sūtra path and one abuses the tantras, or if one's faith is in the tantras and one abuses the sūtras. In any such case of abuse, one incurs this root downfall. One should understand that all of these teachings are from the Buddha, and that they are all methods for attaining enlightenment. Thus, it is improper to abuse any of them. All of these traditions are directed towards the attainment of full enlightenment. In a situation where one thinks, "Oh, my Dharma is good and your Dharma is not good," one commits this downfall.

7. Disclosing tantric secrets to those who have not been ripened.

"To those who have not been ripened" means "ripened through receiving an empowerment." In regard to the Kālacakra, people who have not received the Kālacakra empowerment should not be shown the Kālacakra maṇḍala or the image of Kālacakra himself. One should not explain the meaning of Kālacakra to people who have not received this empowerment. To do so constitutes this root downfall. We will not go into any great detail now, but there is a great danger here. During the empowerment itself, when the initiate stands at the palace, the vajrācārya places the vajra upon the crown of the head and upon the heart, and (with this) binds the devotee to complete secrecy regarding this tantra, saying, "If the secrets are not kept, one's head and heart will burst." This is made very clear during the empowerment itself. At that point in the empowerment, one is also given a drink of water by the vajrācārya who says, "If one keeps the secrets, this water will turn into nectar, which gives rise to siddhis or realizations; but if one fails to do so, it shall turn into the molten iron of the hell realms." This indicates the great danger of disclosing tantric secrets to those who are not fit to receive them.

Question: I have a picture of Kālacakra in my room. Should I keep this covered?

Answer: Yes. It would be better to cover such an image as well as one's vajra, ritual bell and even one's rosary. In the words of Baro Dorje Chang, a recent great lama of Tibet, placing such tantric objects out where everyone can see them is like placing herbal medicine out in the sun. If you leave it out in the sun a long time, the power of the medicine wanes until there is just a shell left. And so, in similar fashion, these tantric implements should be kept hidden. In fact, this is why tantra is most frequently referred to in Tibetan as 'sang ngak' (Tib.gsang.sngags), which means 'secret mantra.' Secret – because one keeps such things concealed.

8. Abusing the aggregates.

It says here in the book [*Kalachakra Initiation, Madison, 1981* (Madison, Wisconsin: Deer Park, 1981), p. 76.], 'your body,' but actually it is the aggregates. Practices such as extreme asceticism, extreme fasting and so on cause the degeneration of one's aggregates. In fact, in the tantric practice, one is purifying and transforming the five aggregates into the nature of the five types of Buddhas. This is what is done in the tantras. Therefore, if one contemptuously regards one's own aggregates, thinking, "These are not fit for such a meditation, this is a waste of time," and with such a contemptuous attitude punishes the body, one then incurs this root downfall.

23

9. *Abandoning emptiness.*

This downfall is incurred by having no belief or by rejecting belief in the lack of inherent existence or lack of true existence of phenomena and thus simply rejecting the point of emptiness.

10. *Devoting oneself to evil friends.*

This refers to very evil people. Specifically, there are four cases mentioned: those who are harming the Buddha; those who are harming the body of the guru; those who wish to harm all sentient beings or have general malice towards all sentient beings; and fourthly, those who wish to bring about a destruction of the Dharma. These are especially referred to as 'evil friends.' One incurs the root downfall by becoming very intimate with such people and devoting oneself to them as one's close friends. This should not be done.

But, in avoiding this root downfall one should, by all means, also avoid the rejection of compassion (Skt. karuṇā; Tib.snying.rje) for such sentient beings because when you reject compassion, you incur another root downfall. Therefore, even though one does not become intimate with, or devote oneself to such people, nevertheless, one still maintains compassion towards them and simply leaves it at that. One can be like a very loving parent who appears to be very wrathful and speaks very harshly to his misbehaving children. In other words, inwardly, the motivation is one of compassion while outwardly, the manifestation can appear to be quite wrathful.

This also occurs in the relationship between a guru and disciple. It is said that it is best when the guru does point out the faults of his disciples. This is one of his duties. It is something he should do. If he does so from his side in order to benefit the disciple and, the disciple from his side, having heard his faults, checks up and acknowledges these and understands them, this is the best possible situation. Being scolded by one's lama is not really a bad thing; it should be understood as an aid to one's own practice.

11. *Not recollecting the view.*

One's obligation in the tantric practice is to direct one's mind to the view three times during the day and three times during the

24

night. If the view of emptiness is with regard to the Prāsaṅgika system, then this should be done. If one is not able to do that, then one can contemplate identitylessness in accordance with any of the following systems: the Svātantrika, the Cittamātra or the Saurāntika [this depends on one's knowledge, abilities and realizations]. But in any case, whatever one is able to do, one should do that three times in the morning and three times in the evening. If one fails to do so, then this incurs a root tantric downfall.

12. Defeating the faith of others.

This occurs when there is another individual who does have faith in the tantric practice and one tells this person "Tantric practice is not much good. It is really gross, with people drinking alcohol," and so forth. If that person then loses faith, or if his/her faith in the tantric practice diminishes, then one incurs this tantric downfall.

13. Not devoting oneself to the tantric pledges.

If, during the gaṇacakra (Tib.tshogs. 'khor), when the meat (Skt. bala) and alcohol (Skt.amṛta) are offered, one says (possibly being vegetarian), "Oh, I am too pure for that, I don't touch meat!"or if one is a monk for whom there is the precept of not taking alcohol and says, "I am a very pure monk and I will not touch that," and in either of these cases rejects the tshog, one incurs this root downfall.

In general, it is true that for a monk who has taken the precepts of renunciation, alcohol is very strictly prohibited. Buddha himself has said that not only members of the monastic community, but even householders should not take even the quantity of alcohol like that of a dew drop on a blade of grass – not even a drop. Therefore, it is generally discouraged for everyone and very explicitly prohibited for monks. Nevertheless, in the context of the gaṇacakra, which is a tantric practice, this offering of bala and amṛta should be taken. One should recognize that there is a special significance in the context of tantric practice, in which the meat is like a hook that brings in the siddhis or the attainments, and the alcohol is like a lamp which illuminates the attainments. Therefore, they have a special significance and the offering should not be avoided out of a notion such as, "I'm a pure monk," or "I am this or that." Actually, an ordained person should just take a drop and a taste, just a tiny amount, not very much. This should be done.

Another example of this root downfall would be thinking, "Oh, I don't need the external mudrās or objects like the vajra, the bell and the hand-drum (Skt. ḍamaru) because the meditation is all inside." Rejecting "all that stuff" and just "meditating inside" – such attitudes and practices would involve this root downfall. In fact, even though there is obviously the internal meditation, still the external implements such as the vajra, the bell and the hand-drum are important. The mudrās are also indispensable, for it is said that if one is practicing Action Tantra and fails to perform the mudrās, the sādhana is incomplete.

14. Disparaging women.

In the tantric context, women are of the nature of wisdom and to disparage them is a root downfall. Particularly in the case where one disparages women in general saying, for example, that women have very heavy mental distortions, they are devious, or that they have unstable minds. This kind of talk and general disparagement must be avoided completely when one enters the tantric paths. [And why?] Because if one disparages women in general, this includes the disparagement of the ḍākinīs themselves. One should rather look upon all women as ḍākinīs.

This completes the presentation of the fourteen general root tantric downfalls. What we have in the book from Madison is the normal presentation of the root downfalls, whereas, the Kālacakra presentation is somewhat different. We should recognize some of the distinctive qualities of the Kālacakara fourteen root tantric downfalls.

ROOT TANTRIC DOWNFALLS ACCORDING TO THE KĀLACAKRA TRADITION

1. Disturbing the mind of the vajrācārya, the tantric master.

2. Breaking the command or the word of the vajra master.

3. Speaking of the faults of a vajra brother or sister [see page 19, No. 3].

4. Abandoning loving-kindness for sentient beings.

Please clearly understand what is meant by loving-kindness and compassion. Loving-kindness is the mind wishing that sentient beings may have happiness [and the causes of happiness]. Compassion is the mind wishing to dispel the suffering [and the causes of suffering] of sentient beings [see page 20, No. 4].

5. Allowing the kunda-like white bodhicitta to emerge.

Kunda is a flower and the white bodhicitta refers to the semen. In the Kālacakra practice, the emission of semen or the white bodhicitta is a root downfall.

6. Making a distinction or discriminating between the emptiness as it is revealed in the Sūtrayāna or Pāramitāyāna, and the emptiness as revealed in Tantrayāna.

Making a distinction in terms of one being better than the other (as if the emptiness taught in tantra were superior to the emptiness taught in the sūtra path) constitutes the root downfall. There is, in fact, no difference whatever between the emptiness taught in one path and the emptiness taught in the other. Where a distinction does occur is in the mind which realizes emptiness. The mind which realizes emptiness through the practice of the sūtra path is a relatively gross mind compared to the mind which realizes it through the tantric path. But in terms of the reality itself, there is absolutely no distinction between the two.

7. Disclosing tantric secrets to those who have not been ripened [see page 22, No. 7].

8. Abusing the aggregates [see page 23, No. 8].
9. Abandoning or rejecting emptiness [see page 24, No. 9].

10 Maintaining a contradiction (hypocrisy) between one's mind and one's mouth in terms of loving-kindness.

In other words, a loving-kindness in which there is a lack of accord between one's mind and one's mouth, that is, speaking very friendly words, with a lot of loving-kindness, while cultivating malice or ill-intent in the mind. This hypocrisy constitutes the tenth root downfall.

11. The eleventh root downfall relates to the circumstances

of the vajrācārya and his consort entering union and, with retention of the white bodhicitta, experiencing the 'supreme immutable bliss' (Tib.mchog.tu.mi.' gyur.ba'i.bde.ba). the lama then explains this experience to the devotee. If the devotee, taking the analogy as simply ordinary sexual intercourse, doubts the validity of that experience, then such a doubt constitutes this root downfall.

12. Directly speaking of the faults of an authentic and fully qualified yogin/yogini or disparaging him/her.

For example, if one should know or see such a being taking a consort and /or alcohol and one disparages such a person, then one incurs this twelfth downfall.

13. Not devoting oneself to the tantric pledge (e.g., not accepting the offering of bala and amṛta during the gaṇacakra or tshog [see page 25, No. 13].

14. Disparaging women [See page 26, No. 14].

This completes the presentation of the 14 root tantric downfalls given in accordance with the Kālacakra tradition. We should understand these very clearly. They are indispensable for the tantric practice. Having understood them, we should diligently avoid committing them.

In order for a root downfall to be incurred, one must have the tantric precepts. If one has not taken them, such a downfall would not occur. The second condition for incurring a root downfall is that one must be in one's right mind. If one becomes mentally disturbed and one of these actions occurs, one does not incur the root downfall.

Apart from rejecting the yearning and the engaging-bodhicitta [the 5th general downfall], all of the other 13 [general] root downfalls must be enacted together with 'four binding factors' for a full downfall to occur. If the four binding factors are not present in the breaking of the 13 precepts, then the root downfall does not occur. What occurs instead is a secondary downfall (Tib.sbom-.po). Consequently, one should be especially careful to maintain one's bodhicitta and prevent oneself from rejecting it.

THE FOUR BINDING FACTORS

1. Not regarding the downfall as disadvantageous or as a fault.

2. Not having the attitude of turning away from such an action in the future.

An example of the second binding factor would be committing the downfall of speaking of the faults of one's vajra siblings with the thought, "There is no fault in this. . . . I'll just carry on in the future doing the same thing."

3. Taking delight in that action, thinking, "That was just great!"

4. Doing so without any sense of shame and having no consideration for others.

Let us try to understand these two phrases: "sense of shame" and "consideration for others." A shameless attitude causes one to fail in avoiding unwholesome actions, taking oneself as the reason. In terms of one's own self-regard, shame is a private or personal matter: "I would not do this action because this is not something I would do." [The opposite is shamelessness.] This may be more clearly understood by understanding the second one, which is "lack of consideration for others." With this attitude, one fails to avoid unwholesome actions, taking others as the reason. For example, considering the Buddhas, the Bodhisattvas or the people around one, one says, "It does not matter what they think. Never mind about them, I'm going to do it anyway." So, on the one hand, it is in relation to oneself, and on the other, it is in relation to others. To engage in a downfall shamelessly and without consideration for others would be the fourth binding factor.

If one engages in one of the 13 root downfalls with all of these four binding factors present, a full root downfall does occur.

In the following explanations we will go on to the eight secondary downfalls (Tib. sbom.po). It is very important to understand them. To follow these precepts and to avoid these downfalls is a very practical form of practice that we should be engaging in.

The Eight Secondary Tantric Downfalls

1. The first of these secondary downfalls (Tib.sbom.po) involves practicing with a consort who does not have the following three indispensable qualities:
a. she must have received the empowerment,
b. she must be abiding in pledges and precepts,
c. she must have trained herself through tantric practice.
It is totally improper to have a consort of just any type whatsoever.

2. Practicing in union without three attitudes:
a. regarding one's body as the deity,
b. regarding one's speech as the mantra of the deity,
c. regarding one's mind as the Dharma (referring to Dharma-kāya).

3. Disclosing or showing objects, such as images of the tantric deities (Hevajra, Kālacakra, Vajrayoginī, etc.) tantric treatises or the tantras themselves, as well as one's vajra and bell, to people who have not received empowerment or to those who have the empowerment but do not have faith in the tantric practice. Furthermore, one should not show the mudrās or the different movements of tantric dances to such people. If any of the above mentioned are shown, one incurs a secondary downfall.

4. Quarrelling during the tshog. A complete assembly (Tib. tshogs. 'khor) for offering the tshog includes both men and women. If there are only men, it is considered a partial male assembly; if there are only women – a partial female assembly. If during any of these three assemblies, either complete or partial, a person speaks argumentative words or quarrels even to the point of striking another person, one incurs the secondary downfall.

It is stated that it is better not to speak at all during the tshog; however, if one does speak, then to speak of Dharma. Apart from engaging in conversation dedicated to Dharma, it is better simply to remain silent.

There is tremendous benefit in performing the tshog. Here in the Sakya Center, thanks to Venerable Dagchen Rinpoche and Dagmo Kusho, you have the opportunity for engaging in it. If it is done properly, there occurs very great benefit. Whereas, if it is done improperly, there can ensue great disadvantages.

5. Deluding or deceiving another person who has faith. This occurs in a case when a person very earnestly asks questions about Dharma and the practice, and although one knows the correct answer, consciously deceives the other person with a false reply. If one simply does not know and, out of ignorance, gives a mistaken answer, that is another matter.

6. Remaining seven days in the home of a Listener (Skt.śrāvaka; Tib.nyan.thos). This specifically refers to a Listener who has contempt for tantra or for tantric practice, one who just writes it off as a waste of time. If, however, there is a purpose, a real need for staying in such a person's abode, then no secondary downfall is incurred.

7. The next secondary downfall occurs when a person, who has done a little bit of tantric practice, maybe the initiatory retreat, a little bit of practice of the stages of generation and completion, thinks that he or she is a great yogin or yoginī, possessing supernatural powers and great insights, and so forth, and announces this to other people.

8. Teaching Dharma to those who have no faith. This specifically refers to giving tantric teachings and instruction to those who have no faith. There are many secret points in the context of tantra which must not be disclosed loosely. To do so involves the eighth of the secondary downfalls.

That was the eightfold group of secondary downfalls. However, there are a few others that are not included in this particular presentation of the secondary downfalls.

One of these additional secondary downfalls is a case in which one has neither done the initiatory retreat (Tib. bsnyen.pa) nor the concluding fire-offering and, without having completed these preliminaries, one:
a. confers initiations on others, that is, leads one's own disciples into the maṇḍala;
b. takes the self-initiation;
c. performs consecration.
If one has not already completed the initiatory retreat and the fire-offering, these three activities are prohibited. If one does any of the three without the preliminaries, one commits this secondary

downfall. This is a very important one and it must be guarded against.

Another additional secondary downfall is transgressing the vows of individual liberation (Skt. prātimokṣa) or Bodhisattva precepts without a specific reason.

That concludes the explanation of the root downfalls and the secondary downfalls which are extremely heavy. Although it is true that the secondary downfalls are lighter than the root downfalls, nevertheless, they are very serious.

COMMITMENTS OF THE NINETEEN PLEDGES RELATING TO THE FIVE BUDDHA FAMILIES

In addition to the above listed downfalls, when taking such an empowerment as we have taken, we also take the commitments of the 19 pledges relating to the five Buddha Families.

1. The Six Pledges Relating to the Buddha Vairocana
The first three are abiding in three types of morality or moral discipline:
a. moral discipline of abiding by one's precepts, be they monastic, Bodhisattva or whatever precepts one has taken;
b. engaging in wholesome, virtuous actions with the motivation of bodhicitta;
c. serving the needs of sentient beings.
The final three are:
d. taking refuge in the Buddha,
e. taking refuge in the Dharma,
f. taking refuge in the Saṅgha.

2. The Four Pledges Relating to the Buddha Akṣobhya

a. The pledge of the 'vajra-mind.' One keeps this pledge when one takes in hand the vajra, which is the external symbol of the actual vajra-mind, and brings to mind the inner vajra-mind which is the wisdom of the indivisible bliss and emptiness. In short, one brings to mind the symbol and the inner vajra-mind together.
b. The pledge of the 'bell-speech' is kept by taking the ceremonial bell in hand and recollecting the wisdom realizing emptiness.

32

c. The pledge of the 'mudrā-body' is kept by generating oneself as the deity, in this case as Kālacakra, and identifying with the deity.

d. The pledge of making the offerings to one's vajrācārya, the vajra master, six times daily.

3. *The Four Pledges Relating to the Buddha Ratnasambhava*

These are the four types of generosity. Before explaining them, one should have clearly in mind that the actual practice of generosity is not the things themselves that one is giving, be it money or anything else. Those are the material substances or the objects of generosity. The actual generosity is the mind, the attitude or intent to give. The following are the four pledges of Buddha Ratnasambhava related to the four types of generosity.

a. Material generosity is the intent to give away material things such as food, clothing, money and so on.

b. Giving of protection or, literally, fearlessness. This involves releasing sentient beings from situations of danger. Here are just a few examples: being able to bring a person out of prison; with other creatures – seeing an insect on a path where it is likely to be stepped on and taking it away from there; or seeing a worm that is out in the sun and, knowing it might get dried up, removing it from the path and putting it in a moist place. Such acts of generosity as these relate to this practice.

c. Sharing or making the gift of Dharma. The greatest benefit occurs particularly when one does so with the motivation of bodhicitta, with great compassion. This is stated by Vasubandhu in his text, *Treasures of Phenomenology*, the *Abhidharmakośa*. He also implicitly states that this should not be done with an improper motivation, such as out of pride or jealousy. It is stated in the sutras that there are 20 benefits from teaching the Dharma with a pure motivation. This is something that can be done not only while sitting on a Dharma-throne; one can be sharing Dharma even while walking about in a park or simply strolling along with another person. If done with a pure motivation, this has such great benefits!

d. Giving of loving-kindness. This is done by repeatedly cultivating loving-kindness, the wish that all creatures might be happy [and have the causes of happiness].

4. *The Three Pledges Relating to the Buddha Amitābha*

   a. Holding the 'outer.' This refers to holding the outer tantras, that is, the first two of the tantric classifications of the Action and the Performance Tantras.
   b. Holding of the 'secret.' This refers to the two higher classifications of tantra – the Yoga Tantra and the Highest Yoga Tantra.
   c. Holding the 'three vehicles.' These are the vehicles of the Listeners, the Solitary Conquerors and the Bodhisattvas. The holding of these three is included in one pledge.

These various aspects of the Dharma should be brought to mind six times daily.

5. *The Two Pledges Relating to the Buddha Amoghasiddhi*

a. Making the Four Types of Offerings

1. The Outer Offering (Tib. phyi' i. mchod. pa).

The outer offerings refer to the offering of objects such as butter lamps, food, incense and so forth. You should not neglect these outer offerings, but should make them in accordance with your present abilities. One can look to the life of the Kadampa Geshe Phuchungpa. Due to his material situation, he was initially able to make only the tiniest of offerings. Gradually, he became more and more affluent until each day he was able to offer 21 pieces of gold. This relates to ourselves as well – it is very practical. A good way to start the day in the morning is to make offerings on your altar. This can be done, for example, with seven offering bowls or, if not seven, simply one. If you have no offerings bowls, then take an ordinary bowl, like a cereal bowl, and offer some water in that. In any case, offer whatever you are presently able. Gradually, your ability to make offerings will increase.

You can make offerings not only of material things but also through the powers of your imagination. You can visualize all

34

kinds of beautiful things. Imagine a greater quantity than you are able to offer materially of the same types of things, such as fruit and so forth. Use the full extent of your powers of visualization. You can mentally offer other things you see around and about – beautiful lights of the city at night, or if you are out walking in the park – offer this. By doing so, you gain the benefits of actually offering these objects.

When the great Kadampa Geshe Potowa was travelling with five or six hundred disciples through a very lovely area, with beautiful meadows and mountains, he simply sat down and offered the *Seven-Limb Pūjā* and praises of bodhicitta. This is a very practical way in which this practice can be followed. Also, by the fact that we are in the constant habit of eating and drinking and that we have to keep on doing it more and more because we have this very strong habit, then whatever we eat and drink, we can offer to the Objects of Refuge. In this way, as the years pass and we are eating and drinking, we can be simultaneously accruing more and more merit.

2. THE INNER OFFERING (TIB. NANG. GI. MCHOD. PA).

In contrast to the outer offerings, the inner offerings are held by one's own consciousness, that is, they are a part of one's own being. The inner offerings are the five meats and the five ambrosias, which are the nectars of one's own being, held by one's own consciousness. The complete act of offering the above involves the following three-fold process:
1) purification of these substances,
2) recognizing and looking upon them as ambrosia,
3) their increase.
Only after one has gone through those three processes, does one make the offering. The inner offering is a particularly important one. In fact, upon giving the empowerment, the lama stresses its importance, saying that one should have the inner offering and that this is the chief of all offerings.

3. THE SECRET OFFERING (TIB. GSANG.BA'I.MCHOD.PA).

This refers to making [a mental] offering of the three types of consorts or ḍākinīs to the lama-yidam, who goes into union with the consort and experiences the wisdom of the indivisible bliss and emptiness. This whole process is the secret offering.

4. THE OFFERING OF SUCHNESS (TIB.MCHOD.PA).

This is made when one looks upon the three factors of the process of the offering:
1) the object of the offering (the objects of refuge, the lama and the yidam),
2) oneself as the offerer, and
3) the offerings themselves.

as existing as mere conceptual imputations, as mere labels, as mere signs and lacking any inherent existence whatever. The offering of suchness involves offering with the understanding called the 'ornament of the view.' One should know that even the lama is lacking in true or inherent existence. We can very naturally (and easily) think that the lama and the yidam (or meditation deity) are truly or inherently existent, especially so when we look upon them as being very fine and think, "This is a very great lama and, therefore, he must be truly existent," or "This is an excellent yidam. . . he/she must be truly existent." This is a mistake. As Gampopa was going up to central Tibet, Milarepa told him, "Look even upon your Guru as being like an illusion." Meaning: look upon the guru as being a mere conceptual imputation, a mere verbal imputation, not inherently or truly existent.

When Milarepa spoke very eloquently of his view of the lack of inherent existence of phenomena, he stated, "There is no meditator, there is no object of meditation, and yet, the Sage (Buddha) states that these are not simply non-existent, but rather exist as conventions." This indicates Milarepa's profound realization of this point. If one just looks at the words themselves, one might take them completely literally and, without the understanding, arrive at the conclusion, "There is no meditator, there is no object of meditation and there is no meditating mind." But, what is meant here is that these three are not inherently or truly existent. Rather, "These and all other phenomena," as the Buddha stated, "do exist as mere conceptual imputations."

36

b. The Second Pledge of Buddha Amoghasiddhi is the General Pledge of Keeping all of the Aforestated Precepts of the Five Buddhas.

This concludes a brief explanation of these 19 pledges relating to the five Buddha Families.

The Three Methods with Regard to Tantric Pledges and Precepts

The Buddha Vajradhara, out of his great compassion, showed three methods with regard to these teachings on the pledges and precepts:

1. the method of acquiring or taking the pledges and precepts for those who have not taken them;

2. the method of preventing the breaking of the pledges which have already been received;

3. the method for restoring broken pledges and precepts.

This method is meant for those practitioners, like ourselves, who are strong in mental distortions and who do commit the downfalls due to mental afflictions, and for those who have incurred the downfalls or broken the pledges. There are three different means within this one method for restoring the degenerated, broken precepts and pledges:

a. The first means for such restoration is going to one's spiritual mentor, one's vajra master, and receiving the empowerment once again.

b. If one is not able to receive empowerment, the second way of restoring the pledges and precepts is to engage in the initiatory retreat together with the concluding fire-offering. Having done so, it is possible to take the self-initiation which purifies the downfalls, the degeneration of the precepts and pledges.

c. If one is not able to apply either of the above recommended methods, then the third alternative is to recite, one hundred thousand times, the purificatory one-hundred-syllable mantra of Vajrasattva. Having done so, the pledges and precepts are purified. This takes quite a while and it is difficult, but it is also one of the techniques.

All of us have received the empowerment, so we should try our best to keep the pledges and precepts that we have taken. If downfalls do occur, we should keep in mind the three methods for purification and try to follow them.

In one's daily practice, one can ward off many potential downfalls if, in the morning, upon arising, one generates one's abode as the maṇḍala of the deity (in this case, the Kālacakra), and while putting on clothes and eating, one blesses the garments, food and drink with the mantra, Oṃ Āḥ Hūṃ.

This concludes a brief explanation of this tantric practice.

THE TWENTY-FIVE MODES OF BEHAVIOR OR DISCIPLINES

The first five are avoiding the five non-virtues/evils:
1. killing
2. stealing or taking that which is not given
3. adultery
4. lying
5. taking alcohol.

The second set of five are avoiding the five 'proximate' or 'secondary non-virtues.'

6. Gambling, such as with dice or playing cards. This needs to be avoided. If one really thinks about this and really follows the disciplines, precepts and pledges of the Kālacakra, it will lend one's life a great dignity.

7. One should avoid eating meat in the three cases of actually seeing, hearing or suspecting that the animal in question was killed specifically for one's own consumption.

8. Idle gossip or letting the mouth run on. Among the so-called ten non-virtues, idle gossip is the least heavy, the least serious. Nevertheless, for beginning practitioners, it is the worst because it is so easy to give up so many hours, so much of one's life, to idle gossip. While one is gossiping, two or three hours can pass with the greatest of ease so that one does not know where the time has gone. In contrast, if we sit for an hour in meditation, it can be tormenting for both the body and the mind. Idle gossip is so easy that one can waste one's life just in that one mode itself. For example, while reciting our sādhanas, we might find a tendency to

fall asleep, but this is never a danger while we are engaging in idle gossip.

9. Mistaken commemoration of one's parents. This has to do with a yearly commemoration of parents who have died by the offering of blood and flesh. Such a false commemoration, or wrong way of remembering one's parents, is to be avoided.

10. Offering animal sacrifices. This was not only a tradition in ancient time, but it also exists today in some places in Nepal and India where, for example, people still kill an animal as a sacrifice and offers its flesh and blood. This is to be avoided.

Abandoning the five types of killing:

11. killing a cow,
12. killing children,
13. killing women,
14. killing men,
15. destroying representations of the Enlightened Body, Speech and Mind. An example for Mind would be a stūpa; for Speech the words of the Buddha, such as the *Kangyur* (collected works); and for the Body of the Buddha would be paintings, statues, and so forth. Thus, destroying any of these constitutes a breaking of this precept.

Abandoning the five angers:

16. rejecting faith in the Buddha and Dharma,
17. having anger towards one's companions,
18. having anger towards one's lord or master,
19. having anger against the Saṅgha,
20. deceiving and misguiding those who have placed their confidence or trust in you.

Abandonment of the five types of attachment are explained quite simply as attachment for:

21. visual form,
22. sounds,
23. smells,
24. tastes,
25. tactile objects that one feels.

This has been a brief presentation of the 25 disciplines, which should be kept according to one's capacity, that is, as well as one is able. However, due to the strong force of mental distortions, conscientiouslessness and lack of awareness, many faults are incurred. In that case, one should not simply disregard or ignore them, but rather recognize the faults, confess them and, when possible, engage in the initiatory retreat (Tib. bsnyen. pa), which makes one fit for the further practice of Kālacakra. Following that, and only following that, it is possible to take self-empowerment, which can purify the harmful imprints that occur due to such infractions.

SECTION THREE

Let us begin by cultivating the proper motivation, aspiring for the highest, supreme enlightenment for the benefit of all creatures throughout space. With this motivation, let us listen to these teachings with the intent of putting them into practice and, upon the attainment of perfect enlightenment, lead all other creatures to that same state.

As has been emphasized before, it is extremely important to know and to keep the various pledges and precepts we have taken because they are indispensable for the practice of tantra, specifically with regard to the stage of generation and the stage of completion. They can be likened to building a house. In order to build a house, first of all, one must have a suitable site. The site, or the ground upon which one will build, can be likened to the proper keeping of the precepts and pledges, on the basis of which one builds the practice of the stages of generation and completion. An explanation of the tantric downfalls and pledges has already been given. Please do not forget them! All of us who have received the empowerment have taken upon ourselves the commitment to avoid these downfalls.

In the words of Ralo Dorje Drag, the great interpreter and tantric practitioner, "Without keeping the precepts and the pledges, there is no attainment of the siddhis. Those who do meditate, but do not keep pure moral discipline, do not know the vital or central point of the practice." Again, please do not forget, but bring them again and again to mind.
[II.]

B. THE EIGHTEEN ROOT BODHISATTVA DOWNFALLS

1. Desiring devotion and fame, one disparages others.

If this happens, the first root downfall occurs and the Bodhisattva precept is lost.

2. *Not giving Dharma and wealth.*

This root downfall occurs in a situation in which one has certain knowledge of Dharma and/or certain material objects which one is able to give away but, out of miserliness, one does not do so when requested.

3. *Not listening, even when there is an apology.*

This occurs when another person has done something against oneself, but afterwards comes with regret to apologize, saying, "This was my mistake. Please forgive me. I apologize." Not listening or not accepting the apology and even responding with greater anger is the committing of this root downfall.

As one listens to these various downfalls, it is important to keep in mind the general context of the Bodhisattva's way of life motivated by the attitude of cherishing others more than oneself. In this context, one should understand each individual precept. Further, it should be understood that a Bodhisattva offers prayers that others might not direct mental distortions such as anger, attachment and jealousy toward himself or herself. This is a very frequent prayer that Bodhisattvas make. One can see how this relates to the downfall here. If one refuses to accept the apology, it is very likely that that person will respond with anger or some other mental distortion, which would be very detrimental for him or her. This is a prayer we too should make - that other people not direct such mental distortions towards ourselves. These prayers do come to fruition, particularly as we draw close to full entlightenment.

4. *The abandoning of Mahāyāna.*

This occurs by abusing or disparaging the Mahāyāna.

5. *Stealing the possessions of the Three Jewels.*

This can be in a very open or direct manner - simply stealing things that belong to the Buddha, Dharma and Saṅgha, or by devious means of trickery or deceit.

6. *Abandoning Dharma.*

This especially relates to the attitude of abandoning the Mahāyāna teachings. Denying that the *Mahāyāna Tripiṭaka*, in particular, are the real teachings of the Buddha incurs this downfall.

7. Stealing the saffron robes.

This involves:

    a. beating a monk as a punishment regardless of whether he is pure in moral discipline or not,

    b. stealing his robes or actually taking his robe away from him,

    c. taking away or robbing him of his ordination.

Any of these three cases involves a root downfall.

8. Enactment of any of the five heinous crimes:

    a. killing one's mother (one's mother in this life),

    b. killing one's father,

    c. killing an Arhat (a Liberated Being),

    d. drawing the blood of a Buddha with malice (not like taking a medical sample, but with a wish to harm),

    e. causing a schism in the Saṅgha. This occurs when one intentionally creates divisions and disharmony among the Saṅgha. It is stated that if one commits this downfall, then even the grass in the area where such a person lives dries up. This last one is a very serious unwholesome act.

If one commits one of these five heinous crimes, even if one tries to meditate for 12 years, no kind of samādhi will arise. It would act as a tremendous obstacle to one's spiritual growth.

9. Holding false views.

This would be holding a view which denies the workings of karma (actions and their results) and of former and later births.

10. Destroying villages or towns.

This comes into question when one has developed supernormal powers, since with them one could destroy an entire city. If one has such powers and uses them to that effect, then one incurs this downfall.

11. Teaching emptiness to those whose minds are untrained.

12. Turning away from full enlightenment.

This occurs when one has already taken the Bodhisattva vow or precept resolving to attain enlightenment for the sake of all sentient beings and has practiced, to some extent, the six perfections. Then, after some time, one grows discouraged with the practice and thinks, "Oh, it does not look like I'll ever be able to attain enlightenment. How will I ever be able to do that?" Turning away from that aspiration and directing oneself rather to the attainment of a Śrāvaka or Pratyeka Arhat, one commits this root downfall. Having taken the Bodhisattva precept, one should maintain one's courage and mental fortitude, keeping a very strong aspiration to serve the needs of sentient beings.

13. *Abandoning the precepts of individual liberation (prātimokṣa precepts).*

Some people who do not understand Dharma or some young people may think that these prātimokṣa vows (such as the monastic vows) are only for people who seek to become Śrāvaka Arhats or Pratyekabuddhas and that they are not for followers of the Mahāyāna. They may consider these precepts unnecessary or of no use. The precepts of individual liberation are, in fact, an extremely important foundation for the entire Mahāyāna path. It is a big mistake to think that these are just for another path. These vows of individual liberation are very highly praised in the Root Kālacakra Tantra.

14. *Holding the notion that through the practice of the Śrāvaka or Pratyeka path it is not possible to completely eradicate such mental distortions as attachment.*

This shows the variety of misconceptions that might arise. Though one might think this, it is certain that through the practice of the Śrāvaka and Pratyekabuddha paths one can completely eradicate these mental distortions as has been proven countless times in the past by great Arhats, such as Śāriputra and Maudgalyāyana.

15. *Speaking falsely.*

What this actually refers to is a situation in which one has not gained realization of emptiness, but makes a pretense of having realized this and tells people, "You must meditate very well on emptiness and if you do, you will gain direct realization like I have." As soon as one utters these words, deceiving others in this way, and the words are understood by them, this root downfall is committed.

44

A downfall occurs in a situation where one is teaching the Dharma and reciting the scriptures to others desiring their devotion and respect as well as a great reputation for oneself. Not admitting this pretention but, instead, maintaining that one's own motivation is pure while pointing to others and saying, "That person over there is teaching out of a desire for devotion and great reputation," one incurs a downfall. It should be clear that this is a downfall, but it is not enumerated among the 18 root Bodhisattva downfalls. It is included implicitly in the first of the 18 root Bodhisattva downfalls - praising oneself and abusing others.

16. The situation in which a person in some position of power, such as a king or a minister, robs the Saṅgha of its possessions.

This could be offerings which are in the temple for the Saṅgha to eat, food that the Saṅgha has, other possessions of the Saṅgha such as their scriptures, or money belonging to the temple. Imagine that a king or some minister robs the Saṅgha of these, then offers them to someone else, say a Bodhisattva. If that Bodhisattva should accept these offerings from the king, he or she commits this root downfall.

17. Imagine a situation in which there is a person who

is very seriously engaged in the practice of meditation, particularly the cultivation of mental stabilization, a patron who wishes to make an offering to this contemplative, and a third person acting as a messenger, who is actually supposed to deliver the offering. Then imagine this messenger not liking the person who is practicing dhyāna; he receives the gifts for the contemplative, but instead of giving them to him, gives them to another person who is simply reciting texts and doing oral recitations. If one does this, one commits the root downfall.

18. Discarding bodhicitta.

These are the 18 root Bodhisattva downfalls. For 16 out of these 18 to occur, they must occur in conjunction with the same four binding factors which were explained previously with regard to the tantric precepts [see page 29]. The remaining two (of these 18) for which the four binding factors are not necessary are:

a. holding false views [see page 43, No. 9], and

b. discarding bodhicitta [see page 45, No. 18].

If either of these two takes place, even without the four binding factors, the root Bodhisattva downfall still occurs.

The 16 root downfalls do not occur in the absence of all four of the binding factors. However, one should not have the mistaken notion that if the four binding factors are absent, there is no fault at all. There is, in fact, a very great fault; it is simply not the complete root downfall. Still, it places extremely unwholesome imprints upon the mind.

This can be likened to another situation in which, let us say, one has a very strong intent to kill someone and maintains that intent but, for some reason or another, is not able to do it. In this case, the full act of killing a human being does not occur. Nevertheless, having that motivation is extremely deleterious to one's own welfare. All of us here, having taken these Bodhisattva precepts and engaging in the Mahāyāna Dharma practice, should keep very well in mind these 18 root Bodhisattva downfalls and guard against them.

There are also 46 secondary Bodhisattva faults. There is no time to go into them now, but it is very important to receive teachings and know them. When the opportunity presents itself, or you make the opportunity, you should try to receive these teachings. Again, be aware of the very fine situation you have here being able to have contact with the great Lama Dagchen Rinpoche. If this were Tibet, it would be very, very hard to meet him personally. Here, it is obviously much easier.

THE THREE METHODS WITH REGARD TO THE BODHISATTVA PRECEPTS

1. The Method for Receiving the Precepts for Those Who Have Not Yet Received Them

One should receive the Bodhisattva precepts from a qualified Mahāyāna spiritual master endowed with the ten qualities and who holds the Bodhisattva precepts.

    a. The mind of such a master should be subdued through the practice of moral discipline [Skt. Śīla; Tib. tshul.khrims].

    b. The mind of such a master is made peaceful through the cultivation of meditative stabilization [Skt. samādhi; Tib. ting.nge.'dzin].

c. The mind of the master is made yet more peaceful through the cultivation of wisdom [Skt. prajñā; Tib. shes.rab].

The first three of these ten qualities involves the master's cultivation of the Three Higher Trainings.

The spiritual master should be:

d. of greater attainment than the disciple,
e. one who enthusiastically serves the needs of others,
f. rich in knowledge of the scriptures. This means that he/she should have received many Dharma teachings.
g. The next quality involves the realization of suchness, that is, the realization of emptiness. If possible, the actual realization should be there or at least a correct conceptual understanding so that it can be taught properly.
h. The spiritual master should be skilled in speaking. This refers to teaching the Dharma. This makes a very great difference in terms of the effectiveness with which the spiritual master can guide the disciples.

Looking to the ancient past in India, it is said that the foremost of teachers was Vasubandhu; the foremost of debators were Dignāga and his spiritual son Dharmakīrti; and the foremost in composition was Aśvaghoṣa. Once Dharmakīrti went to a king who asked him, "Who is the greatest sage in all the land?" Dharmakīrti replied, "The one who is greatest in intelligence is Master Dignāga; the greatest in composition is Aśvaghoṣa; the greatest in rhetoric, in very beautiful writing is Candragomin; but the one who is supreme in all directions is myself." The king replied, "Is it then you who is the greatest in all the land?" And Dharmakīrti said, "You might say so." It can be seen that Dharmakīrti was an extremely self-confident type of person.

He wrote in another verse, "When the sun of Dharmakīrti sets (when he passes away), the Buddha-Dharma will be in a very pathetic situation. It will be as if it were going to sleep or were dying out altogether. Then what non-Dharmic elements will arise and take over?" What he was saying was that after he had passed away, there would come many people disputing the teachings of the Buddha and that there would not be anyone to answer them and defeat them in debate. He was a very fine debator. It is said that he brought approximately 100,000 people to Buddhism.

Still going off on a bit of a tangent (just for fun), looking again at the text *Pramāṇavarttika* by Dharmakīrti, he writes, "All of the rivers find their source in the ocean, and all of the rivers go back into the ocean. Likewise, in this text that I have composed, the *Pramāṇavarttika*, all the reasonings are to be found and these are sent out, but those of weaker intelligence will not be able to understand them. So, eventually all of them will just come back to me again," namely, from the ocean out, and then back to the ocean - himself. In fact, *Pramāṇavarttika* is very difficult to understand. One of his disciples, perhaps his foremost disciple, tried to write a commentary to it and showed one of his first attempts to his Guru, Dharmakīrti, who looked it over and tossed it in the water. Then the disciple wrote a second one. Dharmakīrti looked that one over and tossed it in the fire. The disciple wrote a third one. Dharmakīrti read it, mused for a while, and finally said, "Well, you've gotten the general meaning. It is a good 'meaning commentary' but, as for a word-by-word commentary, you still have not made it." So it is very difficult to understand.

One of the doctrinal advisors of His Holiness the Dalai Lama was Mongolian. He read over the *Pramāṇavarttika* and was so deeply impressed by it that as he was reading, he kept saying to himself, "This man could not be a Cittamātrin!" (Cittamātra is not the highest school of Buddhist philosophy.) Again and again, he would say to himself, "He could not be a Cittamātrin ... He could not be a Cittamātrin." Keeping in mind that Dharmakīrti was a very highly realized tantric master who had visions of Cakrasaṃvara, the Mongolian Geshe stated, "If one looks at the lines of reasoning of Dharmakīrti in the *Pramāṇavarttika*, in relationship to the Cakrasaṃvara Root Tantra, it seems impossible that the author of these lines did not understand emptiness in its final depth of realization."

The great Sakya Panchen, out of his kindness, wrote *Tsad.ma.rigs.gter*, which is a commentary to the *Pramāṇavarttika*, where he very clearly elucidates the thoughts of Dharmakīrti. The same master Sakya Panchen first caused the Buddha-Dharma to flourish in Mongolia, so, he is especially kind in this regard. The life story of the Sakya Panchen is really awe-inspiring to read. To take one instance, while he was once dreaming, he received a complete teaching on Vasubandhu's *Abhidharmakośa* from Vasubandhu himself. When he awoke the next morning, he had complete and profound understanding of the text. In his ordinary appearance he had many such astounding accomplishments as this, but, in actual reality, Sakya Panchen was Mañjuśrī himself.

One account from the life of His Holiness, the present Dalai Lama, is something not often spoken of, and never in public. During the daytime he would be reading the scriptures and, sometimes, he would have some uncertainty or some qualms on certain points. At night he would go to bed and in his dreams all of the points about which he had uncertainty would become clear and the next morning all uncertainty would be gone. There are many other things that are equally awe-inspiring concerning his life too.

Going back to the ten qualities of a fully qualified Mahāyāna master:

   i. The master must be a being of compassion and must particularly have compassion for the disciples.

   j. The master must abandon depression or discouragement. This is specifically with regard to teachings, and more specifically, with regard to teaching very dull-witted disciples with whom the same point will have to be gone over again, and again, and again . . . No matter how often the master has to go over the same points, there never appears any depression or discouragement.

     Here is one example from my own experience. There was a monk who was at the Jhang-guncho, a place in Tibet where monks from the great monastic universities in central Tibet would come to debate on logic and epistomology. Two other lamas and I were simply trying to teach this monk three definitions, the longest being one full sentence. We were three teachers working with one disciple for a period of six weeks trying to teach him the three definitions which are absolute basic fundamentals of logic, and we failed. This, once again, is a case when one needs great perseverance and vigor against depression.

     Another account from the sūtras concerns Ārya Lamchung, who was born of the Brahmin caste and who was, as a youth, trained in the *Vedas*, the Brahmanical literature. However, as much as he was trained he simply did not understand them and his teachers threw him out. He wandered around for awhile, encountered some Buddhists, and studied with an Arhat who tried to teach him the fundamentals of Buddhism. He tried, and tried, and tried but Lamchung still was not able to understand. So, he was taken by the hair and again thrown out. Wandering around, he was thinking, "I am not a Brahmin, and now maybe I am not even a Buddhist. What am I?" While he was wandering around weeping the Buddha encountered him and asked him, "What is your problem? What are you crying for?" Lamchung told him how he was thrown out of here, and chucked out of there, and still did not know anything and was too stupid to learn anything. The Buddha said, "Do not be depressed. The Arhat who tried to help you is a relative of mine but he does not have the same realization as myself. He has neither cleared away all obstructions to full enlightenment nor has he gained the degree of knowledge that I have. I can see that there is still some hope." So, the Buddha took him in hand and taught him two phrases: "Clear out the dust, clear out the stains." When Lamchung memorized "clear out the dust," he could not remember "clear out the stains," and when he remembered "clear out the stains," he would forget "clear out the dust." He could not juggle both in his mind at the same time. Seeing this, the Buddha put him to work in a temple where he would be sweeping out and acting as a servant for the elder of the temple. One day, as he was sweeping he took the broom in hand and understanding [the point] he said, "The actual dust is not the dirt but it is the mental distortions. The actual stains are the mental distortions." By taking the broom in hand he gained direct realization of emptiness, became an Ārya, and went on to become an Arhat.

Taking this as an example, regardless of one's own evaluation of one's intelligence, one should not grow depressed but see that with perseverance and enthusiasm one can progress. Lamchung, also known as Lamten, became one of the Sixteen Arhats. It is said that he became the finest of the teachers among the Sixteen.

Those are the ten qualities of a fully qualified Mahāyāna master from whom one should receive the precepts.

2. The Method for Preventing Degeneration of Bodhisattva Precepts Which Have Already Been Taken

Here is a brief explanation of the 'four black actions' and the 'four white actions.' Through avoiding the former and following the latter one is prevented from being separated from bodhicitta in future lives. It is very important that one maintains this aspiration from life to life. Toward this end it is very important to offer prayers that one may have a continuous cultivation of the awakening mind.

a. THE FOUR BLACK ACTIONS

1) Lying to and deceiving one's spiritual mentor.
2) Discouraging others in their practice of virtue. This can occur when one looks upon another person engaging in Dharma practice and says, "What are you wasting your time on this for when you could be out making money and really having some success?" If one speaks in this way it is a black action - something to be avoided.
3) Speaking unpleasant, harsh words out of anger to a Bodhisattva.
4) Tricking sentient beings out of a motivation other than the superior intent (which is a motivation just preceding bodhicitta).

These are the four black actions to be avoided and should be held well in mind.

b. THE FOUR WHITE ACTIONS

1) Avoiding lying even for the sake of a jest. That is, not lying in order to bring even a laugh.
2) Instilling others not only with delight in their practice, but guiding them towards the Mahāyāna path rather than to lesser paths.
3) Looking upon all sentient beings as being the 'Teacher' (Tib. ston.pa).

4) Dealing very straightforwardly with all sentient beings out of the motivation of the superior intent.

These four points should be clearly understood as methods designed to prevent the degeneration of the Bodhisattva precepts which have already been taken.

3. The Methods for Restoring the Bodhisattva Precepts Which Have Degenerated

Various methods have been designed for the restoration of the Bodhisattva precepts which have degenerated.

    a. One method is to go to one's spiritual mentor and take the Bodhisattva precepts again. In fact, it occurs very frequently that at least some of the 46 secondary faults do occur.

    b. If this is not possible, then one simply visualizes the Buddha and the Bodhisattvas in the space before one and takes the Bodhisattva precepts in their presence.

    c. The third method involves a specific Bodhisattva prayer of confession for the restoration of the precepts.

It is very good that on this Saturday afternoon of this weekend holiday, when you could have been out having fun in the park or having a picnic, you are here having your "picnic of listening to the Dharma" and learning about all the root downfalls. This is far more beneficial.

SECTION FOUR

The mind is of foremost importance since it is through the activity of the mind that one reaches either full enlightenment or one of the lower realms of animals, spirits or hell-beings. One should study and listen to these teachings with the motivation of attaining full enlightenment in the form of Kālacakra for the benefit of all creatures. If one does so, then listening for even five minutes has very great benefit.

One should keep the pledges and precepts as best as one can. Among the precepts and pledges that have already been explained, one should recognize those that one is able to keep now and keep them. For those that one is presently unable to keep, rather than simply discarding them with the thought, "I cannot keep these!" one should recognize one's present inability and offer prayers that, in the future, through the further ripening of one's own mind, one will be able to keep all of them perfectly. In this way, keep them in mind and maintain them as well as possible.

As far as the long-term view of eventually being able to keep all of the precepts is concerned, the mind certainly has this capacity. The Indian Bodhisattva Śāntideva explains in his great text, *The Guide to the Bodhisattva Way of Life*, that the Buddha, whose teachings are true and without deception or deceit, has said that even insects have the ability to attain full enlightenment because they have Buddha-Nature. Consequently, if this is true of insects, it goes without saying that human beings, who are endowed with the ability to recognize and avoid that which is unwholesome and cultivate that which is wholesome, have the ability to attain full enlightenment. If there is the enthusiasm, if there is the effort, then full enlightenment can be attained.

It is a wonderful and rare opportunity to be able to practice tantra because it is so very special. When the Buddha Maitreya appears, the human life-span will be 80,000 years. Buddha Maitreya himself will remain in this world for 60,000 years. During that time he will have an exceedingly great number of Śrāvaka Arhats among his disciples, a far greater number than those who were with the Buddha Śākyamuni.[1] Nevertheless, despite the fact that the Buddha Maitreya will remain so long and have so many disciples, he will not teach tantra. The reason for this is that due to the great degree of pleasure and happiness in that existence, they will neither be inclined toward nor suitable to receive it. The nature of human existence will be very different then. At the present time, however, disciples are very good and fit for tantric practice.

In order to bring one's practice to its culmination, it is necessary to have a constant and evergrowing practice of Dharma. For example, when one is filled with happiness during the good times, one should avoid acting like people who think that because they are feeling good they can do without Dharma. They get happy-go-lucky and carefree, just enjoying the good times, not giving any time to spiritual practice. Instead, one should recognize that well-being is a result of one's former wholesome, virtuous actions. This recognition should impel one to further spiritual practice.

Likewise, there are those who in times of misfortune, be it of poverty, sickness, suffering and so forth, feel, "Oh, I can't practice Dharma now, things are too bad." They are simply too depressed to engage in any practice. This is also a problem. During such times one should recognize misery to be the result of one's previous non-virtuous action and let this recognition impel one to avoid acting in such non-virtuous ways in the future. So, regardless of the situation, one should use it as an aid to one's spiritual practice and, in this way, the practice can proceed to its culmination.

In order to engage in an authentic practice of tantra, as explained repeatedly in the past by such great masters as Sakya Paṇḍita, it is necessary to cultivate the common path. This should be done in the following way: first, focus on the cultivation of renunciation; following this, the generation of bodhicitta; next, the realistic view; then, the stage of generation, bringing to culmination both its gross and subtle aspects; and finally, the stage of completion. This is the manner in which practice should be carried out in order to gain actual realization. Initially, it is essential to recognize that the cultivation of renunciation, bodhicitta and the realistic view are indispensable for the practice of Dharma.

The importance of this point is illustrated in an account of a very great Tibetan lama, Purchog Jampa Rinpoche, who was an emanation of Maitreya. Once, he was giving the Guhyasamāja, Cakrasamvara and Vajrabhairava empowerments in the Jowo Khang, the central temple of Lhasa. On that occasion, Changkya Rolpe Dorje, another extremely erudite lama in Tibet, came to receive the empowerments with a circle of his own disciples, among whom were many well-learned geshes. All of these disciples had gathered there to receive the empowerments and, as the transmission began, Purchog Jampa Rinpoche started by giving a very extensive teaching of the *Lam Rim*, the basic instructions on the cultivation of renunciation, bodhicitta and realistic view. One of the geshe-disciples of Changkya Rolpe Dorje commented [as an aside] that it seemed like Purchog Jampa Rinpoche did not know tantra very well because, instead tof teaching tantra as he should have been doing, he was giving instructions on more fundamental material. But, Changkya Rolpe Dorje put his hands together and said, "The Great Purchog Jampa Rinpoche is a master who combines the qualities of erudition and direct insight, illustrating his profound realization of the very essential meaning of the Dharma. It is because of the indispensability of these three factors that he is stressing them so much." Because they are so vital, many of the Kadampa geshes have said that if one is deficient in these three aspects and engages, for example, in the vase-like meditation on the retention of the breath, it has no more significance than the bellows used for a fire; and even if one is engaging in a very elaborate practice of the stage of generation, it has no more significance than walking around a temple and looking at all the pictures.

To further illustrate this, the stage of generation and the stage of completion are found, in their entirety, in non-Buddhist practices such as the Hindu tantras. Missing in these non-Buddhist practices, however, are renunciation, bodhicitta and realistic view, which are found in Buddhist tantra. Tantra without the three principles of the path is like tü² without butter – it just does not hold together. If one is practicing the stage of generation and completion without bodhicitta, one will not be able to attain even the lower stage of the Mahāyāna path of accumulation. In fact, it will not even be a Mahāyāna practice.

The profound significance of bodhicitta with regard to the practice of tantra can be seen in the life of Atīśa. He had a total of 155 gurus, many of whom gave him tantric empowerments. However, although he had faith in these lamas, above all of them, he had the greatest reverence for Serlingpa, the lama from whom he received the oral transmission of bodhicitta. He had such reverence that whenever he would utter his name he would put his hands together in obeisance and tears would flow from his eyes. This account illustrates how bodhicitta is the very life-force of all Dharma, both the sūtra and tantra practices.

[With the three principles of the path as a foundation,] one should not be discouraged in the practice of Kālacakra, feeling that it is too complicated, too difficult, or that the visualization is too intricate with the different faces, many arms and so on. One should not become discouraged, fall into despair and give up, thinking, "Oh, I'll never be able to do that!" If one becomes accustomed to practicing it, one's ability increases. We can see this in other fields, such as making music or songs and so forth, where people practice, learn the words and, in the course of time, become very adept. If this is possible for music, then it is applicable here as well. Slowly, the ability increases.

Likewise, in the beginning, understanding the meaning of the Buddha's scriptures is quite difficult. It is easy to feel discouraged, thinking that one just cannot understand what is being said. But, if one persists, after a while, one gets a little bit of understanding. And if one goes further and penetrates more deeply, there comes good understanding. Finally, one gains limitless understanding devoid of all obstructions. This was stated by the great Kadampa Geshe Potowa who was one of the three prominent disciples of Dromtönpa and who was said to have been a manifestation of Mañjuśrī.

III. THE MEANS OF CULTIVATING THE PATH

A. CULTIVATING THE STAGE OF GENERATION

MEDITATION UPON THE PALACE – "THAT WHICH IS RELIED UPON" [GENERATING THE PALACE]

There is a tremendous amount of information that could be explained about the nature of the palace, its dimensions and proportions, but this would be a bit too cumbersome for the time being. Therefore, one should simply think of it as being a very glorious place – not at all like an ordinary house. It has four walls, each of which has a door in its center that faces one of four directions. Above each door a golden Dharma-wheel is flanked on either side by a deer.

One should not think of this palace as being made out of stone, mortar, brick and so forth, but rather think of it as being Buddha. In what sense? In the sense that the Wisdom Truth Body of the Buddha manifests in the form of the palace. In other words, the palace is actually an emanation, a manifestation of the Buddha-Mind.

The various parts of the palace are manifestations of facets of enlightenment. For example, the doors to the east, south, north and west are manifesting the 'four close applications of mindfulness,' or more commonly known by the Pāli term as the 'four satipatthānas.' Other aspects of the palace are emanations of the 'four bases of miraculous action,' the 'five powers' and so forth, including the '37 facets of enlightenment'.

Let us practice visualizing it right now and get a bit of an acquaintance with it!

MEDITATION ON THE DEITY – "THAT WHICH RELIES UPON THE PALACE" [GENERATING ONESELF AS KĀLACAKRA]

In the very center of this palace one generates oneself as the deity Kālacakra, standing upon a throne. The visualization of Kālacakra is not generated in front of oneself (Tib. mdun.bskyed). This type of visualization, in which one generates oneself as the deity, is called 'self-generation' (Tib. bdag.bskyed; *bdag* means 'self' and *skyed* means 'to generate'). This is a practice in the stage of generation, the first of the two stages of tantra. It is called the 'stage of generation' (Skt. utpatti-krama; Tib; bskyed.rim) because one is generating the palace and oneself as the Kālacakra deity in that palace.

Kālacakra stands upon a throne of moon, sun, and Rāhu, [and Kālāgni] discs. The color of Kālacakra is blue.

1. He has four faces: one in the front; two on the sides; and one in the back.

The front face is black and in a somewhat wrathful, ferocious aspect so that the eye-teeth are showing slightly. When ordinary people like ourselves get really angry, we grimace and show our teeth. However, such is not the case with a yidam, with Kālacakra. In this instance, the expression appears out of the force of compassion. The ferocity or wrath is not directed toward any sentient being, but rather toward the 'ignorance of grasping at a false identity.' As the great Sakya Pandita said, "Yama, the Lord of Death, kills beings even with a great smile. Whereas, a meditational deity, though appearing wrathful, is actually expressing compassion."

The right face is red and has the appearance of lust or attachment.

The face to the back is yellow with an expression of meditative equipose, as if the deity were in meditation.

The face on the left is white and has a very peaceful expression.

Each face has three eyes, namely, the two [regular] eyes the third 'eye of wisdom.'

2. The hair on the head is coiled into a topknot on top of which is a varicolored vajra with the symbol of the half-moon. In addition, the deity is adorned with many jewel ornaments, such as the ornament on the very crown of the head, the necklace, the earrings, the ornaments on the wrists and ankles and so on. Finally, the deity is dressed in a tiger skin.

3. There are 24 arms, 12 on either side. The first four arms are red, and the last four arms are white.

The first of the right black arms embraces the consort and holds a vajra in the hand; the second – a sword; the third – a trident (like that of Īśvara); and the fourth – a cleaver.

The first of the right red hands (or the fifth hand) holds an arrow, which is called a 'fire arrow' in the text, but it is simply an arrow. The second red hand holds a long-handled vajra hook which, on its upper end, has a half-crossed vajra on one side and a hook on the other. The third hand holds a damaru (hand-drum) which is producing a drumming sound. And the fourth hand holds a hammer.

The first of the right white hands holds a wheel; the second – a spear; the third – a stick; and the fourth and final of the right white hands – an axe.

These are the 12 right hands with their respective implements and they should be kept clearly in mind.

The first of the left black hands holds a bell; the second – a shield. This type of shield was used in the past to guard against arrows and swords when fighting sword-battles. However, if you look at the thanka printed in the book, the illustration is a bit strange because the shield is down. Actually, the shield should not be held down facing oneself but should be held outward to help you a bit. This incorrect way of depicting the hand holding the shield down and facing oneself was done repeatedly. A number of artists in Dharamsala (India) were painting the deity in this way. His Holiness the Dalai Lama noted how they were painting it and said "Now, you take a shield and hold it like that! Wouldn't your hand be vulnerable to spears and swords?" They were very impressed by his practical wisdom and, I guess, eventually caught on. In any case, it is indeed a shield, but the way of holding it is a bit backward.

In the third left black hand, the deity holds a khaṭvāṅga. This is a certain kind of staff that has three skulls and half-crossed vajra impaled on it. It is the same type as the one held by Cakra-saṃvara.

In the fourth, the deity holds a skull-cup (Skt. kapāla) filled with blood.

Now we go to the red arms on the left. The first hand holds a bow, the second – a lasso, which is not used today. In the past and in Tibet as well, when a couple of people were having a fight they would bring out a lasso, snag the other person and then "beat the dickens out of him." The third hand holds a precious jewel; and the fourth – a white lotus.

The first of the white hands on the left holds a white conch; the second – a mirror; the third – a vajra or an iron chain; and finally, the fourth – the head of the deity Brahma, by the hair.

4. Kālacakra has only two legs. The right one is red and the left one is white. There is much significance to this which will gradually be explained. Simply stated, the right leg symbolizes the right energy-channel (Tib. ro.ma) which is filled with blood, and the left leg symbolizes the energy-channel on the left (Tib. rkyang.ma) filled with the white bodhicitta. There is much more that could be said but we will leave it at this very simple explanation for the time being.

5. The consort of Kālacakra is called Natsog Yum (Tib. sna.tshogs.yum). *Yum* means 'consort' [or 'mother']; thus, the Natsog Consort. She is yellow in color and, likewise, has four faces, each with three eyes: the front one is yellow, the one on the right is white, the one on the back is blue, the one on the left is red.

6. She has eight arms – four to the right and four to the left.

The first of her right hands, the arm of which embraces Kālacakra, holds a cleaver; the second – a vajra hook; the third – a drumming ḍamaru, like that of Kālacakra; and the fourth – a rosary, which she is turning/counting.

The first of her left hands, the arm of which embraces Kālacakra, holds a skull-cup filled with blood; her second hand on the left holds a lasso; the third – a white eight-petalled lotus; the fourth – a precious jewel.

7. Natsog Yum is wearing a crown, which is of the nature of Vajrasattva. She is adorned with the five types of ornaments, whereas Kālacakra himself has six types of ornaments. The missing ornament on the consort is the one symbolizing the white bodhicitta. Her left leg is in union with the deity Kālacakra.

It is very important to clearly understand the significance of the sexual union of the deity and consort. It very specifically symbolizes the union of method and wisdom. In this case, the deity Kālacakra symbolizes method which, in this tantric context, refers to the great bliss. The consort symbolizes wisdom which is the

60

realization of emptiness. Their union symbolizes the union of the great bliss and the wisdom realizing emptiness.

The further meaning is that without the wisdom of the indivisible bliss and emptiness, it is impossible to reach the state of full enlightenment. It is for this reason that Kālacakra, symbolizing the method, and the consort symbolizing the wisdom, are in union. Hold this very clearly in mind!

This is a full form of the Kālacakra deity with the 24 arms and his consort, Natsog Yum, with eight arms.

We should realize the great good fortune of being able to generate, or to meditate on ourselves as a Buddha. We have never done so before and, although we are not Buddhas at the moment, it is legitimate for us to engage in such a meditation because we are cultivating the identification with the deity that we will become – the resultant Buddha. Eventually, we will actually attain the state of Buddhahood, manifesting as Kālacakra. To that end, we are identifying with and drawing that into the present. With this identification we must cultivate the divine pride of being the deity, Buddha Kālacakra, that we will become. So, the two (the visualization and the pride) go together. We should meditate on this and do our best.

If you are not able to engage in this visualization in the detailed way, you can generate yourself as the deity in the simple form, having one face and two arms, holding the vajra (right) and bell (left). The consort holds a cleaver in her right hand, a skull-cup in her left.

However, at the beginning you should not expect the visualization to be clear. It will not be! So, while generating or visualizing yourself as Kālacakra, you can visualize yourself as the generally blue deity in union with the generally yellow consort; vaguely imagine the palace around you, hold it in mind and be satisfied with that. You should not immediately expect a very precise visualization, that comes only through practice. This is not only true for meditation but it is also true for sculpting, painting and so on. At the beginning one has to be satisfied with a crude attempt but, in the course of practice, one's skills increase. Eventually, in this meditation we gain a very powerful experience of both the pride and the visualization of Kālacakra.

The great tantric master, Gungtang Rinpoche, was once giving the oral transmission of the tantric deity Vajrabhairava. Among those receiving it was a disciple with very, very good powers of visualization. In the course of the teachings, he was visualizing himself in the form of Vajrabhairava with many arms, each hand of which was holding some implement. At that point he was asked to be a tea-bearer. He was a young monk and when he was told to pour the tea for people, he looked around in confusion and asked, "But how shall I pour tea? All my hands are full!?" Of course the Lama responded, "Just use your hands . . . these right here!"

I hope that this will not create any great difficulties for us when we have generated a strong visualization of Kālacakra and try to get into the automobile to drive, but cannot get to the steering wheel because all of our hands are full.

NOTES

[1]Another distinction between the Buddha Maitreya and Buddha Śākyamuni is that Buddha Maitreya will be much larger physically. A Buddha always appears somewhat larger than ordinary people around him. In general, during the time of Maitreya, human beings will be larger and, in turn, Buddha Maitreya will be even larger. The environment will also be quite different: it will not be mountainous or rough but flat.

[2]Tü is a very tasty Tibetan dish made from cheese, brown sugar and butter. It is butter that holds the ingredients together.

SECTION FIVE

First of all, we should cultivate a proper bodhicitta motivation, the awakening mind aspiring for full enlightenment for the sake of all sentient beings. With this aspiration, we listen to teachings with the intent of putting them into practice thereby attaining full enlightenment in the form of Kālacakra and leading other sentient beings to the same attainment.

[III. A. CULTIVATING THE STAGE OF GENERATION]

THE MEANS OF ENGAGING IN THE MEDITATION

It is far more important to gain a clear understanding of the meditation than to go into the intricate details of the specific implements, what they mean, as well as the many details of the palace and the maṇḍala of Kālacakra. If one is able to meditate on the full form of Kālacakra with the four faces and the 24 arms, this is fine. However, it is very difficult. If, on the other hand, one finds this practice beyond one's [present] ability, then, for the time being, one should meditate on oneself as Kālacakra in his simple form with one face and two arms.

There are two aspects of the meditation ('divine pride' and 'clear appearance') directed toward eradicating ordinary conceptual grasping and ordinary appearance.

1. Divine Pride

The first point to emphasize in the meditation is cultivating the 'divine pride' (Tib. lha'i.nga.rgyal), the pride of identifying with the Buddha Kālacakra that one will become. It would be a mistake

63

to think, "I am a Buddha," while one is not a Buddha; however, the divine pride in this practice is based on the fact that one will eventually attain full enlightenment in the appearance of Kālacakra. This is called 'taking the fruit and applying it to the path,' that is, taking up the fruit of one's spiritual path, which is oneself as a fully enlightened being, and applying it to the present point in one's own spiritual path. Hence, one is identifying with the Buddha one will become and applying this in the present. Therefore, first of all, cultivate the pride and keep this strong and stable in the mind.

2. Clear Appearance

When there is some sense of stabilization, you can further develop the 'clear appearance,' involving the visualization in some detail, going through the dark and white parts of the eye, and then down through the various parts of the deity. But first and above all, seek stability. Furthermore, at the outset of the meditation, when one is just beginning and one's capacity is not very great, it would be best to just focus upon the front black face only. If even the whole front face is a bit too much, on the basis of having already cultivated divine pride, it would be better to focus on just the one wisdom eye.

3. Aspects of the Practice Leading to the Attainment of Clear Stillness

As one engages in the meditation, one must seek mental stability and beware of and eradicate what are called the 'five faults,' One accomplishes this by means of the 'eight remedies' which are aspects of the practice leading to the attainment of 'clear stillness' (Skt. śamatha; Tib. zhi.gnas).

Such an accomplishment in this Kālacakra practice would lead to the attainment of the gross and subtle stages of the stage of generation. It is by this means on the tantric path that one attains clear stillness. Maitreya, in his text *The Investigation of the Center and the Extremes* (Skt. *Madhyāntavibhāga;* Tib. *dbus.dang- .mtha'.rnam.par.'byed.pa)*, taught these five faults and eight remedies, which are equally applicable whether one is following a sūtra or a tantra path.

a. THE FIVE FAULTS

1) The first of the five faults one encounters in the practice of meditation is called 'laziness' (Tib. le.lo). In the practice of Kālacakra, it is simply the lack of interest or desire to meditate; more specifically, to generate oneself as Kālacakra. This type of laziness is the first fault.

2) The second fault is literally called 'forgetting the quintessential teaching' (Tib. gdams.ngag.brjed.pa). It does not refer to forgetting teachings that one has heard or received from the lama, but rather to forgetting the object of the meditation while trying to meditate upon oneself as Kālacakra. One's mind no longer stays involved with the image or the visualization of oneself as Kālacakra and simply wanders elsewhere. Consequently, it is actually forgetting the object of meditation.

3) The third fault has two aspects called 'sinking' and 'excitement,' both of which come under one heading (Tib. bying.rgod). They are the two chief obstacles in the course of meditation which must be eradicated.

'Sinking' is a very literal translation. There are two types of sinking: gross and subtle.

When the mind is very steadily abiding on the object, but the clarity of the mind is missing, this is 'gross sinking.' One does not have to be concerned about gross sinking until one is rather advanced in the meditation since it only occurs when there is stability.

The nature of 'subtle sinking' is such that, although stability and clarity exist, vivid clarity with extra vitality and strength do not. This happens because the retention of the mind is a bit too loose, too slack. Subtle sinking occurs when one is quite advanced in meditation. So advanced, in fact, that the scriptures relate how many Tibetan lamas arrived at this point where they were subject to subtle sinking, but failed to see it. Failing in this way, they thought they had attained some extremely high tantric realization or, perhaps, the state of samādhi on the stage of completion.

To sum up [when subtle sinking occurs], although clarity exists, the real vivid clarity of the mind, which needs to be cultivated, does not. This is an extremely subtle obstacle that needs to be recognized [and eliminated] eventually.

Grosser than either of the two types of sinking is 'mental fogginess.' This is the cause of sinking and is much more obvious. We can experience mental fogginess now as it simply involves a heaviness of both the body and the mind.

For the time being, when one is just beginning in this type of meditation, one really does not need to worry about sinking, and especially about subtle sinking. The reason for this is that sinking only occurs when there is a strong mental stability, that is, when the mind really abides with the object.

Since, in the early stages of the meditation, the mind is so rambunctious and has so much agitation, this fault will not arise. Progressing toward the attainment of clear stillness, one passes through nine mental states. It is not until one has gained the fifth state that subtle sinking occurs. Even gross sinking will only occur around the fourth of these mental states. Before then, there is so much agitation that subtle sinking is simply not a matter of concern.

The second of the two major obstacles in the course of meditation is what is technically called 'excitement.' Again, there are two types of excitement: gross and subtle.

'Gross excitement' occurs when the mind is agitated or distracted and, consequently, simply loses the object. In other words, it veers off the object and goes elsewhere, so that the object is althogether lost. It is relatively easy to recognize.

'Subtle excitement' occurs when retention of the object exists simultaneously with an undercurrent of rambling thoughts. Is the object there? Yes. Is the mind focused on the object? Yes. However, some kind of rambling thoughts are also occurring, for example, "I would like to go off on a drive," or "When the meditation is finished, I have to do that," and so on. This subtle agitation/excitement is rambling thought beneath the surface of the meditation, like water flowing beneath the ice on a river.

Sinking and excitement must be eradicated. If they are not dispelled, it is neither possible to achieve a really fine samādhi nor to arrive at the culmination of the stage of generation. As already mentioned, only through the culmination of the stage of generation in this tantric practice does one attain clear stillness. In brief, clear stillness is only reached on this high level and it cannot be attained without dispelling sinking and excitement.

4) The fourth fault is 'non-application' (Tib. 'du.mi.byed). It occurs in a situation when either sinking or excitement arises and there is a need to apply the appropriate remedies to dispel these faults, but one neglects and fails to do so. Thus, one does not apply the necessary remedies. This non-application is the fourth fault.

5) The fifth fault is called 'application' (Tib. 'du.byed). This fault occurs in a situation in which one has already recognized sinking and excitement, has already applied the necessary remedies, has already dispelled these faults such that the mind is now free of them, and yet continues to apply the specific antidotes for sinking and excitement. In other words, once one is free from these faults, one should no longer apply the specific remedies for eliminating them. If one does so at such an inappropriate time, this then damages one's mental stability. This fault would be that of application.

One should clearly ascertain and keep these well in mind because such faults as these arise in meditation and one needs to be able to recognize them when they occur.

b. THE EIGHT REMEDIAL APPLICATIONS

The first four remedial applications are specific antidotes for dispelling the first of the five faults, laziness.

1) The first of the remedial applications is 'faith' (Tib. dad.pa). One can speak here of faith in samādhi, the development of concentration or, more specifically related to this practice, faith in the Kālacakra stage of generation. Such faith is generated by recognizing and having confidence in the tremendous benefits one gains through cultivating the stage of generation.

2) The second is 'yearning' (Tib. 'dun.pa), which actually involves an aspiration or striving toward the object of the faith [in the Kālacakra stage of generation].

3) The third remedial application is 'enthusiasm' (Tib. brtson. 'grus).

4) The fourth is called 'suppleness' (Tib. shin.sbyangs). In fact, among these four, the direct antidote for laziness is suppleness. However, the three preceding aspects of faith, yearning and

enthusiasm are the mental faculties that give rise to suppleness, which then acts as a direct antidote to dispel laziness. The word 'suppleness' has a very specific meaning here and we need to differentiate between physical and mental suppleness.

● When 'physical suppleness' arises, one actually feels a physical ease, a physical lightness and a physical readiness similar to a sense of physical well-being. The body is fit for action, fit to be used as one chooses. It is a fit tool.

● When 'mental suppleness' arises, the clarity of the mind, the clarity of the visualization becomes very strong. One's mind is filled with a great sense of mental well-being and gladness, a sense of mental well-being and gladness, a sense of mental and physical buoyancy (sometimes shin.sbyang is translated as 'buoyancy'). Whether one wants to engage in meditation or recite prayers, whatever one might wish to do, the mind is there, ready for action. This quality of suppleness is attained through the cultivation of samādhi or concentration.

5) 'Mindfulness' (Tib. dran.pa) is the mental factor or capacity of the mind to retain the object or the qualities with which the mind has become accustomed. In this case, it is the mental factor that retains the visualization of the face [of the Kālacakra deity]. That is its function or duty.

It is the direct antidote for what has been called 'forgetting the quintessential teachings,' forgetting the object of meditation. This occurs when the power of mindfulness, involving retention of the object, wanes and the mind wanders away.

To draw an analogy, it is comparable to driving down the freeway. You keep your eyes and your mind right on the freeway. You do not wander off to the left or to the right because you would increase your chance of a collision. In like fashion, while you are doing this meditation, whether you are focusing on the general body of Kālacakra or on his face or simply on the wisdom eye, keep your mind right on that and do not allow it to veer to the left or to the right. It is actually a fairly close parallel.

When you drive, you also keep an eye out to the right and to the left in order to make sure you will not get cut off by traffic on either side. Likewise in meditation, you keep your attention focused on the main object, but in the meantime you look to the right and to the left to see whether sinking or excitement are arising. You keep on guard for them.

A quote from one text states, "As long as I am not able to focus my mind, even for the time it takes to milk a cow and my mind is flying off in this and that direction without being able to retain mindfulness, it is impossible to progress along the 'grounds' and 'stages' of either the sūtra or tantra paths. Therefore, I will apply myself assiduously to the practice of meditation.* Bless me that I may do so!"

Special emphasis is on this point: "I shall assiduously address myself to this practice." It is not just a matter of relying on the great blessings of the Buddhas. If this were the case, we would already be fully enlightened ourselves. Rather, it is half and half. One half - the effort we exert from our side; and the other - the blessings from the Buddhas.

One meditator in retreat was giving much time to meditation. But, as he was meditating, he would occasionally break his session and tell his servant, "Oh, I want this," and in a little while, "Get me that." The servant, a bit confused, asked, "What is all this coming from the meditation?" To which the novice meditator replied, "I have so much time to think while sitting in meditation that I remember all the things I had forgotten I wanted you to do for me!" Mindfulness is considered the crucial factor in meditation - if it is really firm and stable, samādhi can be attained quite easily.

6) The sixth of the remedial applications is 'introspective alertness' (Tib. shes. bzhin). Its function is to check up on the mind. It is called 'introspective' because it does not concern itself with the visualization, but with observing the mind, which is visualizing. "Is the mind on the visualization? Is it focused there or is it wandering?" While one part of the mind retains its object through mindfulness, it is the mental factor of introspective alertness which checks up on that mind. One might actually find during the meditation that, sometimes, the mind goes off to town or off driving and so forth. When introspective alertness sees that the mind has wandered off, it brings the mind back in and applies it again to the meditation.

*This refers especially to the stabilization of the mind and the cultivation of clear stillness.

69

In other words, introspective alertness is initially necessary in order to recognize and ascertain the presence of faults. Once it has done so, one is then in a position to apply specific remedies for the faults. And how does this function? While the main force of one's attention is focused upon the object of meditation (here, oneself as Kālacakra), literally 'one corner of the mind,' or one part of the force of the mind, is turned back on the meditating mind itself in order to determine whether the mind is focused on, or veering off the object. Therefore, it is the 'quality control' for the meditation, checking up to see whether or not the mind is meditating properly.

If introspective alertness discovers that a fault has arisen in the meditation, then one applies specific remedies to dispel the fault in question. For example, if sinking has arisen, one needs to apply specific remedies that inspire or exalt the mind.

To draw an analogy, in war one needs to reconnoiter in order to discover if the enemy is present or attacking. This would be your spy. The spy is not the main force of your army but is out there, peeking around to see if the enemy has arisen or not. If he checks and sees that the enemy is attacking or is present, then the spy does not go out and wage war with him; he goes back to headquarters and tells them about it and they do what is necessary. In like fashion, introspective alertness is just one aspect of the mind. It does not go and try to eliminate the faults, it simply recognizes them. One must then apply specific remedies.

Mindfulness and introspective alertness are two factors that must be cultivated because of their extreme importance. By doing so, one gradually arrives at a greater stability in the meditation. In the beginning, however, there is not much stability. Nevertheless, the Buddhas of the past reached enlightenment by training their minds in this way. At one time, they too were like ourselves and they did not start out with glorious accomplishments. But, through practice such as this they reached their goal.

7) The next remedial application is that of 'application' which is the antidote for non-application. When sinking or excitement arise, one needs to refrain from non-application and apply the necessary remedies.

Sinking occurs due to the vitality of the mind going too low. As a result of this, one needs to apply remedies to uplift, exalt and inspire the mind in order to give it more energy. This can be done, for example, by contemplating the preciousness of one's own human existence, the great potential and great fortune of meeting the Buddha's teachings, the opportunity of cultivating bodhicitta and, in various ways, inspiring the mind. When the mind is uplifted from this kind of low energy level, lifted up to a more usable, appropriate level, then, setting aside the remedy, one goes ahead with the meditation.

Excitement occurs when there is too much energy, too much tension. In this case, one needs to lower it, to subdue it, make it more workable. For example, one would meditate on such topics as impermanence, the sufferings of the lower realms of existence and so forth. It is a fault, in general, to have too much energy, to be, in a sense, too glad all the time. If one is "blissed out" all the time, has a lot of energy and is always excitedly happy, then this acts as an obstacle to the meditation.

There is the account of the king Śuddhodana, whose position was such that he was always very glad and would reflect upon his great fortune. Sixty thousand of this Śākya clan had attained great realization on the Buddha's path and he was completely blissed out over this fact. In the meantime, he was not gaining any direct realization himself. On one occasion, when the Buddha was giving teachings, many devas and the Four Great Kings were present but, somehow, King Śuddhodana was not admitted. Suddenly he was very downcast and depressed.

When the exaltation of his mind diminished, it became ripe to receive teachings and he, too, gained realization.

8) The eighth remedial application is 'non-application.' In a situation in which sinking and excitement have been dispelled, it would be a fault to apply remedies to dispel that which does not need to be dispelled. Therefore, the antidote is not to apply any remedies or applications, but simply to carry on with the practice of samādhi itself.

Just as in school, one passes successively through different grades, so too does the gradual cultivation of samādhi lead to clear stillness. In the context of the tantra and generating oneself as the simple form of Kālacakra, one's first task is to prevent the mind from being dispersed, that is, to draw it in and focus it upon the object - oneself as the simple form of Kālacakra. This entails the attainment of the first of the nine mental states (Tib. sems.gnas.d-gu) which is called, 'mental placement.'

c. THE NINE MENTAL STATES

1) At the beginning of the meditation, one cultivates the first mental state, 'mental placement' (Tib. sems.' jog.pa). At this point, the mind has very little stability; one finds the object and then very swiftly loses it. The mind wanders elsewhere. Thus, it is going out and being drawn in again and again. When one actually engages in the cultivation of clear stillness, eventually one feels that, as a result of meditation, one has more wandering thoughts than before. It seems that the meditation is increasing mental distraction. When this recognition occurs, one should not regard it as a fault, but rather as a good sign that one now has a greater awareness of what is happening in the mind.

To draw an analogy, one might be outside somewhere and, as long as one is not paying any special attention but is simply sitting there with a wandering mind, daydreaming about this and that, one would not necessarily notice if many cars or people pass back and forth. One would not especially notice, or even know, whether or not a lot of traffic passed by because one would not be concerned. But if, one another day on the same spot, one really paid attention to the number of people and cars passing by, one would notice a great deal of traffic. One might conclude, "There is a lot more traffic today than before," whereas, in fact, there is not. At this time, instead of being oblivious one is being aware.

2) The second of the nine mental states preceding and leading to the attainment of clear stillness is called the 'continual placement' (Tib. rgyun. du.'jog. pa). Before this attainment, one continues practicing a great deal and, again and again, brings the mind in after it has wandered off. Eventually, sufficient stability does arise in the mind so that the attention will remain uninterruptedly focused on the object for, say, five, six or seven minutes. When that degree of stability has been attained, one has reached the second mental state called continual placement.

3) The third mental state is called the 'patch-like placement'

(Tib. glan. te. 'jog.pa). With the attainment of this third state, one's degree of mental stability is even greater than before such that the mind will remain uninterruptedly focused on the object for, say, 10–15 minutes. It is called 'patch-like placement' because, basically, the mind is focused upon the object with a reasonably good degree of stability and yet, occasionally, it will wander off. On those occasions, one recognizes this and brings it back. One is 'patching-up' one's samādhi. This is similar to having a tear in one's robe – one recognizes it and says, "Oh, there!" and just patches it up.

4) The fourth mental state is called 'close placement' (Tib. nye.bar.' jog.pa). Having attained this fourth state, the mind no longer loses the object of meditation, because the power of mindfulness has come to completion. This is similar to a person growing up. There will be certain physical tasks that can or cannot be performed. However, when this person becomes an adult of 20 years or so, his strength is complete and he is now able to do whatever is necessary. In like fashion, the strength of mindfulness is now complete. One does not lose the object, because the mind is no longer drawn away from it.

5) The fifth mental state is called 'subduing' (Tib. dul.ba.byed-.pa). While one is abiding in the previous mental state of close placement, the mind becomes very inwardly directed and a high degree of stability exists. But, on the basis of that attainment, a very great danger of subtle sinking exists as well. For this reason, one especially needs to cultivate an extremely acute introspective alertness. It has to be extremely acute, because this fault of subtle sinking is very, very subtle and difficult to recognize. In fact, many contemplatives of the past have mistaken a concentration in which subtle sinking has arisen with proper and extremely fine samādhi. They stunted their practice by failing to recognize the fault of subtle sinking and thought, instead, that they had accomplished their goal.

To draw an analogy, if one is in a household in which the other people in the house are lavishing one with kindness, praise, nice words and so forth while, at the same time, they are robbing one blind, it is very difficult to recognize them because they seem to be one's friends. They are much more difficult to recognize than people who come pounding on one's door as blatant robbers or bandits. Those, at least, are easy to recognize. In like fashion, subtle sinking can very easily be mistaken for proper meditation, whereas, in fact, it is a fault which must be recognized. It is recognized through an extremely acute introspective alertness.

6) The sixth mental state is called 'pacification' (Tib. zhi.bar-.byed.pa). While abiding in the fifth mental state, the subduing, which is, in fact, a very fine degree of samādhi, one is giving a lot of effort or attention to cultivating extremely acute introspective alertness. As a result of this, the energy of the mind increases a great deal. With this increased and perhaps excessive energy of mind, as one goes to the sixth mental state, there is a danger of subtle excitement. To guard against this, one needs to recognize it by means of very active introspective alertness.

7) The seventh mental state is called the 'full pacification' (Tib. rnam.par.zhi. bar.byed.pa). In this state, there is not really much danger of the arisal of either sinking or excitement. They will occasionally arise a little bit and, when they do, they are not difficult to dispel and can be eliminated by the force of enthusiasm. By and large, they are not there. In the illustration of an elephant following a winding path, depicting the course of mental development towards the attainment of clear stillness, at this stage, the elephant, representing the mind, has a little tiny bit of blackness on it symbolizing the fact that the mind, at this point, is only slightly subject to sinking and excitement.

Here is a recent example of Geshe Rabkye, who was in the same class with me. In cultivating clear stillness, he had definitely attained the seventh of these nine states. In his meditation for two or three hours at a stretch, he would have impeccable concentration, a very high degree of samādhi. At that point he died. However, if he had lived, there seems no doubt that he would have proceeded right to the full attainment of clear stillness. Once one has attained the seventh state, to attain the following ones is a matter of relative ease.

When I was in Dalhousie (another hill-station in northern India) quite a few years back, I was living alone very, very simply with only the most basic possessions. At that time, compared to Geshe Rabkye, I was very wealthy. He really looked simply like a beggar;

all he had was a meditation cushion, a couple of pictures and that was it. Sometimes Geshe Rabkye, who was very good in debate, would come to my place and talk or debate. Once I asked him what realization had he gained and he replied, "Well, I have not gained any real realization, but I have the feeling no one in the world is happier than I am." This is an indication that he was truly a spiritual practitioner. His Holiness the Dalai Lama really took a very special interest and had an especially great affection for Geshe Rabkye. He invited him down from the mountain, where he was meditating, into his own palace to meditate there. It is true that His Holiness the Dalai Lama does take this very special interest, have this special affection for people, be they Tibetans or Westerners, who are devoting themselves very earnestly to spiritual practice.

8) The eight mental state is called 'single-pointed application' (Tib. rtse. gchig.tu.byed.pa). Upon the attainment of the eighth mental state, sinking or excitement no longer arise. By this time, at the beginning of one's sitting session, with just the slightest bit the effort, the mind becomes focused upon the object (in this case, oneself as Kālacakra). One can then simply continue to abide in the meditation for as long as one likes. For the duration of the meditation, there is no sinking or excitement. This can be likened to a person who falls asleep and is completely out for eight hours, sleeping solidly the whole time without any effort. Likewise, with just a little bit of effort at the beginning of the sitting, this person can sit for a long time during which sinking and excitement do not arise.

9) The ninth mental state is 'even-placement' (Tib. mnyam.par. 'jog.pa). With the attainment of this state, one is totally accustomed to the practice. Without any effort at all, one simply enters the meditation, focuses upon the object (oneself as Kālacakra) and abides in it effortlessly. This is like a person who has recited the Oṃ Maṇi Padme Padme Hūṃ many, many times. It becomes so effortless that, even if his mind is wandering all over the place, his mouth is saying Oṃ Maṇi Padme Hūṃ, Oṃ Maṇi Padme Hūṃ. . .

Even at this point, however, one has not yet reached the actual state of clear stillness. This is called 'single-pointed concentration of the realm of desire.' One needs to continue in the meditation and, after some time, there arises a very special kind of joy and bliss, so strong that it is almost unbearable. It arises, and then it wanes a little bit. Thereafter, there arises a physical joy due to physical suppleness, and then a joy due to mental suppleness. It is following this that one actually reaches the attainment of clear stillness, also called the 'access concentration to the first mental stabilization.' Once one has attained this state, the mind is an extremely fine instrument for any type of meditation one wants to engage in. The mind will simply be able to focus on that. And that is that!

These are the nine states one gradually passes through, regardless of whether one is practicing the sūtra or the tantra path. The way one progresses (whether focusing on the face or merely on an eye) is by focusing and maintaining mental stability with good mindfulness for, say, five minutes, gradually extending to ten, then fifteen mintues and, in this way, lengthening the period of stability further and further.

If one truly tackles this type of meditation, it necessitates full use of one's intelligence to approach it in a variety of skillful ways. Sometimes, one will be sitting in meditation, intensely applying oneself while, at other times, one needs to relax. Then again, at other times, one needs to apply oneself toward accumulating merit and purifying unwholesome imprints and obscurations. And why? Through the meditation in which one cultivates clear stillness, one chiefly accrues 'collection of wisdom,' sometimes called 'mental merit'; whereas, through other practices, for example, devotional practices such as performing the *Seven-Limb Pūjā*, as well as through cultivating generosity and so forth, one chiefly accumulates 'physical merit' or 'collection of merit.' Therefore, through meditation one is accumulating only the mental merit.

If one is accumulating only one type of merit, this can create an imbalance that can produce insurmountable obstacles. For example, if one is just engaging in meditation, as many people nowadays think is possible, this causes an imbalance which can create simply one obstacle after another. And why? Because with a deficiency of [physical] merit, it is possible that disturbances of one's subtle winds or other obstacles might arise. In fact, even

76

though one is not using up merit through meditation, but is actually accumulating mainly the collection of wisdom, it might seem as if one were exhausting it. The reason for this is that if one is just focusing on and cultivating this one type of merit, which is also very much related to wisdom and intelligence, it is said that this can decrease one's lifespan. When disturbances and obstacles of this type arise, one needs to focus more on the accumulation of [physical] merit and purification of unwholesome imprints, accomplished through performing complementary practices such as the ones mentioned above, the *Seven-Limb Pūjā*, making offerings and so forth.

However, if one already has a tremendous store of merit, the situation can be different; but, nowadays, we are beings living in what is called the 'time of degeneration.' So, we must balance our meditation or complement it with these other practices [designed specifically for the accumulation of physical merit]. Otherwise, because one obstacle will come after another, it can perhaps seem as if one were exhausting one's merit. In brief, one must have a balanced practice, comprised of meditation and complementary practices, that is, one must accumulate both physical and mental merit [in order to attain one's goal].

d. THE SIX POWERS

1) The first among the 'six powers,' by means of which one attains the nine mental states, is the 'power of hearing' (Tib. thos.pa'i.stobs). It is by means of the power of hearing and retaining the master's instructions on the meditation that one attains the first of the nine mental states.

2) The second is the 'power of thought' or the 'power of reflection' (Tib. bsam. pa'i. stobs). It is by means of this power, which involves thinking or reflecting upon the teachings one has heard and bringing them to mind again and again, that one goes on to attain the second mental state.

3) The third is called the 'power of mindfulness' (Tib. dran. pa'i. stobs). It is by means of this power that one attains the third and the fourth mental state.

4) The fourth is the 'power of introspective alertness' (Tib. shes.bzhin.gyi.stobs). With this especially acute power of intro-

spective alertness, one is on guard, first against subtle sinking and then against subtle excitement. Thus, by means of this power, one attains the fifth and sixth mental states.

5) The fifth is the 'power of enthusiasm' (Tib. brtson. 'grus-.kyi.stobs). Remember that it is in the seventh state that one dispels the occasionally arising sinking and excitement by the power of enthusiasm. Then in the eighth, at the outset of the sitting, with just a little bit of effort and a little bit of application of enthusiasm, one can continue unhindered.

6) The sixth is the 'power of full acquaintance' (Tib. yong. su. 'dris. pa'i.stobs). It is by this power that one attains the ninth mental state. By this time, one effortlessly engages in the meditation because one is habituated and accustomed to the practice.

Just as one uses different methods to build a house or an airplane, so are these six powers the tools for building the structure of clear stillness. In fact, this practice can be included in the field of knowledge of creativity, which was mentioned previously. Among the three aspects of this field - physical, verbal and mental creativity - this practice is included in that of mental creativity.

e. The Four Types of Attention

Now we go on to the four types of 'attention' which are also means for attaining these nine states.

1) The first of these is called the 'squeezing attention' (Tib. bsgrims. te. 'jug.pa'i.yid.byed), or forceful attention. It is with this attention that one attains the first two mental states.

2) The second attention is the 'interrupted attention' (Tib. chad.cing. 'jug.pa'i.yid.byed). It is with this type of attention that one attains the third up through the seventh mental states. It is called 'interrupted' because it is during this period of mental cultivation that one's concentration is interrupted by the occurrence of sinking and excitement.

3) The third is the 'uninterrupted attention' (Tib. chad. pa.med.pa. 'jug.pa'i.yid.byed). This occurs in the eighth mental state.

4) The fourth is the 'spontaneous attention' (Tib. lhan.gyi.grub-.par. 'jug. pa'i.yid.byed). It occurs in the ninth mental state.

This is the means for the practice of meditation and these are the teachings. Whether one actually applies them or not is one's personal affair. However, whether or not one does engage in the practice of meditation, simply listening to the teachings and ascertaining their meaning leaves extremely beneficial imprints on one's own mindstream. One finds in the sūtras many such accounts including those of Maudgalyāyana and Śāriputra. Both of them practiced a great deal during the time of the Buddha Kāśyapa, the Buddha before our Buddha Śākyamuni. But, although they practiced a great deal, they did not become Arhats at that time; so, both of them offered prayers that they would attain Arhatship during the time of the next Buddha, the Buddha Śākyamuni. In that lifetime, with a short period of practice, they attained a very great realization and became Arhats very swiftly. In like manner, if we can meditate, this is excellent. Nowadays though, people are very busy; one might simply not find or make the time for a lot of meditation. Do as much as you can! Merely receiving the teachings is very beneficial. Due to their imprints and through the merit stored in this way, it can happen in the future that with very little effort, with just a few conditions coming together, one may attain samādhi very, very swiftly.

This is the manner in which one generates oneself as the deity Kālacakra. As Sakya Paṇḍita said, "one generates oneself as one's special tutelary deity, and by doing so, dispels the ordinary appearances and conceptualizations. Through this, one rises from the cycle of existence. By the elimination of ordinary appearance and conceptualization, one opens oneself to the tremendous blessings of the Buddhas and Bodhisattvas." We should, by all means, listen to the words of this great master.

Sakya Paṇḍita continues, "By this means, one purifies unwholesome mental imprints accumulated with the body. One should continually recite the mantra of Kālacakra, which acts to purify unwholesome mental imprints accumulated through speech. One should cultivate compassion in union with the realization of emptiness to purify unwholesome mental imprints accumulated through mental activity. In this way, if one purifies the unwholesome imprints accumulated through the body, speech and mind, there is no way that one can avoid becoming a fully enlightened being."

79

Moreover, Lama Gungtang Jampeyang said, "The door which opens the Dharma is hearing the teachings and reflecting upon them. A person who turns away from the bounties of the cycle of existence, particularly of this life, has the quality of the one who is holding Dharma. Thus, turning one's back on the pleasures of this life alone, and looking beyond to the hereafter is the distinction between a Dharma practitioner and one who is not. And finally, the essence of the path is method and wisdom and the union of the two."

The teachings on the nine states and the four attentions come from Asaṅga and his texts the *Grounds of the Listeners* [Skt. *Śrāvakabhūmi*; Tib. *Nyen. thos.kyi. sa*] and *Bodhisattva Grounds* [Skt. *Bodhisattvabhūmi*; Tib. *Byan.chub.sems.sems.dpa'i.sa*]. The teachings on the six powers, by means of which one attains the nine mental states, have been explained by Holy Maitreya and are found in the *Ornament for the Mahāyāna Sūtras* [Skt. *Mahāyāna-sūtrālaṃkāra*; Tib. *Mdo.sde.rgyan*, one of the five works of Maitreya brought back from Tuṣita Heaven by Asaṅga]. In brief, the teaching which has been given here comes from Asaṅga and Holr Maitreya. It is said to be the king of quintessential instruction on the cultivation of clear stillness.

In addition to the above teachings, the author Asaṅga describes, in his *Grounds of the Listeners*, the 13 accumulations which are the causal accumulations toward the attainment of the clear stillness. Je Tsongkapa, in his *Exposition of the Stages of the Path to Enlightenment* (Lam.rim.chen.mo), highly recommends this text to people who are following this type of meditation. Therefore, it should be read and studied. It is especially beneficial to read texts written by Asaṅga and attributed to Holy Maitreya: *Ornament for the Mahāyāna Sūtras* [mentioned above], the *Investigation of the Center and the Extremes* [Skt. *Madhyātavibhāga*; Tib. *Dbus. dang.mtha'.rnam.par. 'byed.pa*], the *Ornament of the Realizations* [Skt. *Abhisamayālaṃkāra*; Tib. *Mngon.par.rtogs.pa'i.rgyan*] and others. By doing so, as His Holiness the Dalai Lama has said, one places imprints upon the mind.which lead to one's future rebirth in the circle of the foremost disciples of Maitreya.

If you want to meditate, the teaching that has been given here is indispensable. The sources of the teachings are the Buddha himself, the Holy Maitreya and Asaṅga. From such totally authentic spiritual guides, there is no possibility that one could be deceived or follow mistaken paths. Understand them and then meditate to the best of your abilities. This meditation practice is for students as well as for teachers. Therefore, I encourage you to meditate and I will do the same.

That is all for today. Everybody now has plenty of things to meditate on. You should be very clear about these teachings. There is no time now to go downtown shopping . . . from now on, meditate only!

SECTION SIX

We should listen to these teachings on the Kālacakra with an awareness of the great good fortune of having the opportunity to receive them. In addition, our listening should be free of the three faults of a vessel:

having a mind which is like an upside-down pot;

having a mind which is like a pot with holes in it;

having a mind which is like a pot that is dirty inside.

Finally, we should listen with the three types of attitudes or six recognitions[1], as well as with a cheerful mind and a glad countenance.

[III. A.]

TAKING THE THREE BODIES OF THE BUDDHA AS THE PATH

The task in the Kālacakra practice is to purify and transform ordinary death and ordinary birth. Other tantras, such as Guhyasamāja, Vajrabhairava and Hevajra, speak of the purification and transformation of death, intermediate state and birth as a means toward enlightenment. In the Kālacakra Root Tantra, there is no reference to purifying the intermediate state; it speaks only of purifying death and birth. However, the very process of purifying ordinary death and ordinary birth automatically purifies the ordinary intermediate state. While still on the path and not yet a Buddha, by this means, one attains a facsimile of the three Bodies of the Buddha which take the nature of the actual three Bodies of the Buddha upon full enlightenment: the Truth Body (Skt. dharmakaya; Tib. chos. sku), Enjoyment Body (Skt. sambhogakaya; Tib. longs.sku) and Emanation Body (Skt. nirmāṇakya; Tib. sprul.sku).

In this tantric practice, there are the two stages: the stage of generation and the stage of completion. The function and the task

82

of cultivating the stage of generation in general is to purify the ordinary birth, death and intermediate states. What is meant here by 'an ordinary state' is one that occurs due to mental distortions and actions motivated by mental distortions. That is what is to be purified.

It is indispensable to attain the stage of generation prior to the stage of completion, because it is impossible to attain the realizations of the stage of completion if one has not yet attained the stage of generation. It is like taking one step before the next. Step two is out of the question unless step one has been achieved. In Tibet, this was a subject of much disputation. Some lamas held the mistaken view that the stage of generation was directed only towards the attainment of mundane siddhis such as psychic powers.

A paraphrase of the definition of the stage of generation is as follows:

It is a deity yoga in which the energies, or winds (Skt. vāyu; Tib. rlung) have not yet entered, abided and dissolved in the central channel by the forces of meditation. It is a yoga which is a ripener for its resultant stage of completion to which it leads. In other words, it ripens one's mental continuum for the following stage of completion and bears a similar aspect to birth, death and the intermediate state.

Very briefly stated, in the actual death process, there occurs the gradual dissolving of the elements: the earth dissolves into the water; water into fire; fire into the wind; and the wind dissolves into the consciousness which, itself, goes through ensuing experience in the death process. What is the meaning of ". . . a similar aspect to . . ."? In the course of the meditation on the stage of generation, although one is not dying yet, the meditation one engages in is similar to the death process, as well as the subsequent processes of the intermediate state and birth. That will have to be a sufficient explanation for the time being.

Crucial to the stage of generation is taking the three Bodies of the Buddha as the path. Through cultivating the stage of generation by applying these aspects (of taking the three Bodies of the Buddha as the path), one cultivates the causes for being able to die without the suffering of fear. In fact, if one becomes adept in this practice on the stage of generation, as a result of becoming very acquainted with it, one transcends any fear of death. As Milarepa said, "It was fear of death that drove me to the mountains. There, I meditated upon the deathless nature of mind. Now, death holds no fear for me." Although there is no question of the fact that we will eventually die, through such a practice, one can be freed of any fear of death. Again, to paraphrase Milarepa's statement, he likens the Lord of Death to the shadows cast by a mountain. As the sun goes down, the shadow comes closer and closer and closer – you take one step away from it, it takes one step towards you; you take another step, and it just keeps on following you until, finally, it catches up. It is the same with the Lord of Death who approaches without cessation. He is not just another person standing there, such that you can walk away and leave. Therefore, he is likened to this ever-advancing shadow. However, Milarepa says, "Having attained enlightenment myself, I am now free of this danger," and he encourages us to follow [the path leading] to the same attainment. These teachings of Milarepa are extremely fine, extremely nice to hear, as well as having profound importance.

Following death, the intermediate period occurs in which there is normally much fear. Such a practice [of taking the three Bodies of the Buddha as the path] enables one to pass through the intermediate state without fear, and also to take birth free from suffering.

There are many meditation manuals describing practices on the stage of generation. Some of these are very brief, but if they are complete in the practice of taking the three Bodies of the Buddha as the path, they are a complete practice. Even though other meditation manuals or guides are very long in dealing with the stage of generation, if they miss any of the three aspects of taking the Bodies of the Buddha as the path or applying them to the path, they are not a complete guide.

1. TAKING THE TRUTH BODY OF THE BUDDHA AS THE PATH IN CONJUNCTION WITH ORDINARY DEATH

In order to follow the first of these three, taking the Truth Body of the Buddha (Skt. dharmakāya; Tib. chos.sku) as the path, one first needs to gain a clear ascertainment of what are called the 'three fundamental' or 'basic bodies' (Tib. gzhi'i.sku.gsum) [death, intermediate state and rebirth]. The term 'fundamental' or 'basic' refers to the time while one is still in the cycle of existence.

DISSOLUTION OF THE TWENTY-FIVE GROSS FACTORS

Each of us is endowed with 25 gross factors or aspects which need to be dissolved in the following practice. These 25 are: the five aggregates, the four elements of earth and so forth, the six sense faculties, the five sensory objects, and the five transcendental wisdoms. One is born with these 25 and they gradually dissolve during the death process. Moreover, it is important to recognize the five aggregates and their relationship to the five transcendental wisdoms and the five types of Buddhas. At the time of one's attainment of enlightenment, these five aggregates are of the nature of the five Buddhas.

1) *Aggregate of Form*

There are five qualities relating to the form aggregate (Skt. rūpa; Tib. gzugs):

a) The first is the form aggregate itself.

b) The 'fundamental mirror-like wisdom' refers to the mind in the present state, which is able to perceive many objects simultaneously, just as a mirror is able to pick up many images simultaneously.

(The term 'fundamental' or 'basic' refers to the time while one is still in the cyclic existence.)

c) The third quality relating to the form aggregate is the earth element.

d) The fourth quality is the eye faculty [sense].

e) The fifth quality is the form which is held by one's continuum.

There are five outer signs of the dissolution of the form aggregate occurring during the death process:

a) Even if the body is normally quite heavy, it becomes thinner, decrepit and loses its strength and power.

(b) The sign of the dissolution of the fundamental mirror-like wisdom is that one's visual perception become hazy or indistinct.

85

(c) The sign of the dissolution of the earth element is that the body feels very heavy, the limbs become very slack and one feels as if one is buried under the ground.

(d) Normally, the eye-lids flicker. The sign of the dissolution of the eye faculty is that the eyes become still, glazed over, taking on lifelessness. In short, the life goes out of the eyes.

(e) The sign of the dissolving of the form which is held by one's continuum is that the complexion or radiance of the body diminishes and becomes very poor.

These are the outer signs of death occurring during the death process and people who are nurses or aides to the ill would understand them.

While the outer signs can be seen by a person observing the dying, there are inner signs that occur [while one is passing through the death process], which take place in one's own subjective experience.

• The first corresponding inner sign that occurs simultaneously with these outer signs during this stage of the death process is the 'mirage-like apparition' that appears to the mind. This is comparable to being out in the desert when the sun is shining down on the hot sand and seeing an apparition or mirage of, for example, water that is not actually there. Likewise, there occurs a mirage-like apparition during this stage of the death process.

2) *Aggregate of Feeling*

There are five qualities relating to the feeling aggregate (Skt. vedanā; Tib. tshorba):

a) The feeling aggregate itself. Feeling is the mental factor which experiences suffering, happiness and indifference.

b) The 'fundamental even-minded wisdom' is the mind or cognition which remembers the three types of feelings: pleasant, unpleasant and indifferent.

c) The water element.

d) The ear faculty [sense].

e) The sound which is held by one's continuum.

There are five outer signs of the dissolution of the aggregate of feeling occurring during the death process:

(a) The sign of the dissolution of the feeling aggregate [itself] is that the feelings associated with the various sense conscious-nesses vanish, namely, they no longer arise.

(b) The sign of the dissolution of the fundamental even-minded wisdom is that one is no longer aware of the feelings associated with the mental cognition.

(c) The sign of the dissolution of the water element is that the tongue becomes very dry so that one is not able to speak very clearly and can only mumble very inarticulate sounds. Also, the various fluids within the body, such as the blood, perspiration and the seminal fluid, dry up.

(d) The ear faculty dissolves so that one no longer hears sounds.

(e) The fifth sign involves the dissolution of the inner sound which is held by one's continuum. Normally, we can hear a subtle humming in the head. At this point, however, this inner humming or droning sound stops.

● The corresponding inner sign that occurs simultaneously with these outer signs is what is called the 'smoke-like apparition.' This is not like the smoke seen billowing up from a fire, but rather more like the smoke in a room where incense has been burning - a still haze of smoke.

3) *Aggregate of Discrimination*

There are five qualities relating to the aggregate of discrimination (Skt. saṃjñā; Tib. 'du.shes):

a) The aggregate of discrimination is the mental faculty which is able to recognize or distinguish different people, like one's mother, father and so forth. It is the distinguishing or recognizing faculty of the mind.

b) The 'fundamental discriminating widsom.'

c) The fire element.

d) The nose faculty [sense].

e) Smells which are held by one's own continuum.

There are five external signs of the dissolution of the aggregate of discrimination occurring during the death process:

(a) With the dissolution of the aggregate of discrimination itself, one no longer recognizes the meaning of different objects. In other words, one is not able to distinguish or recognize different realities.

(b) The sign of the dissolution of the fundamental discriminating wisdom is that one is no longer able to recollect the names of different objects or people - one's father, mother and so forth.

(c) The sign of the dissolution of the fire/heat element is that the warmth of the body is lost, the body becomes cold. If the heat recedes from the body, going from the feet up, this is an indication that one is about to take rebirth in a fortunate realm. Whereas, if the heat recedes from the head down, it indicates that one is about to take birth in a lower realm. In any case, the heat gradually does come together at the heart. The consciousness also abides here for some time. At conception, the consciousness is first at the nucleus of the heart. Likewise in the death process, the final abode of the consciousness in the body is at the heart. This is where the final heat would be.

(d) The sign of the dissolution of the nose faculty is that the exhalation of breath is quite strong, but the inhalation is very, very weak.

(e) The sign of the dissolution of the smells which are held by one's continuum is that one is no longer able to smell any type of fragrance.

• As far as the inner sign is concerned, there occurs an apparition like 'fireflies in the sky.' To understand this, it would be like lighting a bundle of grass, setting it on fire, and then tossing it into the air, with sparks flying in different directions. It could also be compared to hitting a log that is on fire and seeing the sparks fly.

4) *Aggregate of Mental Formations*

There are five qualities relating to the aggregate of mental formations (Skt. saṃskāra; Tib. 'du.byed):

a) Sometimes, 'mental formations' is translated as 'volition,' which is one of the mental formations. In any case, this aggregate is that faculty of the mind which enables us to move. It emphasizes the volition aspect of moving the limbs, moving from one place to another.

b) The 'fundamental accomplishing wisdom' is that faculty of the mind which impels us into various types of ordinary worldly actions, and recollects those actions, as well as the purposes involved in them.

    c) The wind element.

    d) The tongue faculty [sense].

    e) Tastes which are held by one's continuum.

There are five outer signs of the dissolution of the aggregate of mental formations:

    a) The sign of the dissolution of the aggregate itself is that one is no longer able to move intentionally, that is, to move the body or to apply one's volition to physical movement.

    b) The sign of the dissolution of fundamental accomplishing wisdom is that one no longer recollects actions or their purposes.

    c) With the dissolution of the wind element, there is the complete cessation of breathing or respiration, such that an ordinary, worldly person would think, "Oh, this person is now dead."

    d) With the dissolution of the tongue faculty, the tongue itself becomes very thick and the root of the tongue, the base, turns blue. One is no longer able to speak.

    e) The sign of the dissolution of the tastes which are held by one's own continuum is that one is no longer able to taste any of the six types of tastes [sweet, sour, bitter, astringent, pungent and salty].

At this time, the tactile faculty or tactile organ and the physical sensations which are held by one's continuum dissolve. The sign of this is that one no longer feels any type of tactile sensation, be it of softness, coarseness and so forth.

• The inner sign that occurs at this time is called the 'butter-lamp-like apparition.' In some texts, this is described as an inner vision or apparition like a fluttering candle when it is going out and is sputtering. My own teachers say that this is not quite correct. Rather, it is more like an apparition of a very still and constant flame, like a butter-lamp or a candle, which is guarded by a paper shade. It is very still and very faint, giving constant radiance. So, the apparition is more like this.

This has been a fairly elaborate description. It relates to a process that many of us have probably heard of, where one speaks of the earth element dissolving or merging into the water element, which then dissolves or merges into the fire element, that into the wind element, and that into consciousness. These relate to the same process, but one should understand the terminology here. When we say, for example, that the earth element dissolves into the water, this is not to say that the earth element transforms into the nature of the water element, which then transforms into the nature of the fire element, and so on. Rather, what it means precisely is that the earth element, which is acting as the foundation for consciousness, and is supporting consciousness, loses its power to do so. And due to the loss of the potency of the earth element, the water element becomes more apparent, appears more clearly. It seems as if one dissolves into the other, but, in fact, that is not the case. One does not become of the nature of the next.

5) *Aggregate of Consciousness*

By the time the above signs have occurred, such a person would normally (in the world) be pronounced dead; acutually though, the person is not yet dead. There are a number of apparitions or experiences that are yet to be passed through before the actual death, such as the experience of a 'pale light,' 'reddish light' and of 'darkness.' This becomes much clearer in the explanation of the stage of completion.

In order to understand this, first of all one needs to know that the white bodhicitta [the white drop obtained from the father] is normally held in the cakra of the 'great bliss' (Tib.bde.chen. 'khor.lo) by the knots in the channels (Skt. nāḍī; Tib. rtsa), as well as by the 'life-supporting wind' (Skt. prāṇa; Tib. srog. 'dzin. gyi. rlung). Normally, this is the case. A great yogin, who is advanced in this practice, will be able to unravel the knots of the channels and bring down the white bodhicitta, passing through these stages [of dissolution] consciously by the force of his meditation. But in the death process this occurs naturally. By this time in the death process, the life-supporting wind has already receded from this area and has come back to the heart, no longer upholding the white bodhicitta there. The knots in the channels become unravelled and the white bodhicitta descends. Where it descends to is called 'the drop which is indestructible

for the duration of life' (Tib. ji.srid. 'tsho .yi.bar.du.mi.shig-
.pa'i.thig.le).This is quite small in size and is located right now
at one's heart. In the death process, the wind and the
consciousness converge into this drop at the heart. This term,
'the drop which is indestructible for the duration of life,' occurs
very frequently in tantric texts.

There is yet another term (Tib. brtan.du. mi.shig.pa'i.thig.le)
which means 'the forever indestructible drop,' referring to the
'extremely subtle consciousness and energy' or 'wind' inside the
drop which is indestructible for the duration of life. These
forever indestructible components are so called because they are
indestructible throughout this life, through death, through the
intermediate period, through the full duration of one's existence
in the cycle of existence, and right on through to one's
attainment of enlightenment and, following that, as an Enlightened Being. The extremely subtle energy and consciousness
remain throughout; they are totally indestructible.

a) *The Four 'Empties'*

   (1) For the reasons previously explained, at this stage in the
       death process the white bodhicitta descends to the drop
       which is indestructible for the duration of one's life and
       covers the top of it. During this descent, one has an inner
       subjective experience of an apparition or vision of pale
       light, like the moon just rising from beneath the horizon,
       casting a pale sheen upon the sky.[2]
       The inner mental consciousness during this first stage is
       called the 'mental consciousness of appearance' (Tib. snang.
       ba'i.yid.shes). At this time, there occurs the first of the four
       'empties' (Tib. stong.pa.bzhi) which is called the
       'appearance-empty' (Tib.snang.ba. stong.pa) [or just 'the
       empty' (Tib. stong.pa)].[3]

   (2) Following this, the mental consciousness of appearance,
       together with the accompanying energies, dissolves into the
       'mental consciousness of increase' (Tib. mched.pa'i. yid.
       shes). The inner sign during this occurrence is a reddish-like
       light apparition. The empty that occurs at this time is called
       'the very-empty' (Tib. shin.tu.stong.pa).[4]

91

Do not try to draw the meaning from the above names. The meanings are as follow: the life-supporting energies have [already] retracted from the upper parts of the body, and the white bodhicitta has descended. Likewise, they are retracted from the lower portion of the body beneath the heart and are drawn up into the heart. As a result of this, the red bodhicitta [obtained from the mother], the female element residing at the navel,[5] is no longer held down, but rises and also comes up to the indestructible drop at the heart.

(3) Following this, the mental consciousness of increase, together with its corresponding energies, dissolves into the next type of mental consciousness, the 'mental consciousness of near-attainment' (Tib. nyer.thob.kyi.yid.shes). What occurs at this point is that the red bodhicitta and the white bodhicitta now completely cover the indestructible drop at the heart, like a shroud. The inner experience at this time is one of darkness, like on a very, very dark night when there are no stars, there is no light.

With this type of mental cognition, there occurs the 'great-empty' (Tib. stong.pa.chen. po).[6]

There are two phases of the experience of the mental consciousness of near-attainment in which the experience of darkness occurs. In the earlier phase, there is the experience of darkness. In the latter phase, there is simply no awareness at all, a lack of awareness. By this time, there is a cessation of the specific consciousnesses and energies that were developed in this life.

(4) Following this period of a total lack of awareness, a period of tremendous mental lucidity arises as the extremely subtle consciousness and energy become manifest. There is an extraordinary mental clarity. This can be likened to an extremely clear, bright and radiant sky, free from any type of blemish, any clouds.[7] At this time, one does not realize emptiness, but the mind is endowed with such a tremendous degree of clarity that it might seem like it. This experience is called the 'clear light of death' (Tib. 'chi.ba'i. 'od. gsal). It is a very common term that one encounters frequently in

tantra. What is manifesting at this time is the continuum of the extremely subtle consciousness and energy that carries on right to our own Buddhahood and thereafter. This, then, is the fourth empty, 'the completely-empty' or 'all-empty' (Tib. thams.chad.stong.pa).[8]

b) *Clear Light*

At this point in the death process when there occurs this period of great lucidity, the extremely subtle energy and consciousness, called the 'mother clear light' (Tib. ma'i.'od.gsal), become manifest. A highly advanced tantric practitioner or a yogin can also arrive at a similar state through meditation, that is, not in the death process, but simply during meditation. This is called the 'son clear light' (Tib. bu'i.'od.gsal). When entering into the actual death process and applying the wisdom that is cultivated through meditation to his own death process, such a practitioner integrates the mother clear light and the son clear light so that there is the combination of the two. When this occurs, such a yogin or yoginī may abide in this state during the death process for even a year or two or sometimes just for weeks.

What has been called here the 'clear light of death,' and which occurs for any person, is not the actual clear light. It is often mistaken as such, but it is not the actual emptiness, not the actual clear light. However, for an advanced tantric yogin or yoginī, who combines and thus manifests the mother and son clear light, the clear light that is experienced during his death process is the actual clear light.[9] One should remember this distinction and know that it is not true that any sentient being, upon reaching this point in the death process, experiences the actual clear light.

Upon the conclusion of the experience of the clear light of death [see p. 92 (4)], the consciousness departs from the indestructible drop and one's existence in the intermediate state commences.

Signs of this are that the white bodhicitta, which was at the heart, being of the nature of water, descends and emerges from the genital organ; whereas, the red bodhicitta, the female element which is of the nature of fire, ascends and appears from the nose, like a little drop of blood. These outer signs do not occur for every person at death. But in cases when they do, it is certain that death has occurred, that consciousness is no longer in the body, and one can then burn the body or dispose of it as one likes. However, if one disposes of the body before the death process is completed, there is a great fault in this - one accumulates the karma of killing because the being is still alive.

b. MEDITATION PRACTICE WHICH PARALLELS THE DEATH PROCESS

The practice relating to this process is called 'taking the Truth Body (Skt. dharmakāya; Tib. chos. sku) as the path.' This is a meditation practice on the stage of generation in which the basis to be purified during the practice is ordinary death. As one engages in this practice, one follows a sequence of meditation which parallels the process of death that has just been explained.

One could generate oneself as Kālacakra and emits rays of red light in all directions, which strike the environment and sentient beings in the environment. Transformed into light of the nature of great bliss, these then dissolve back into one's own body, into oneself. At this time, one should imagine that there occurs the experience of the mirage-like apparition [see p. 86].

In the next stage of the meditation, one's entire body (the top, bottom, front and back) transforms into light. Then, the light dissolves into the Hūm [pronounced 'hoong'] syllable at the heart. This visualization is better done with the Tibetan letter. At this point, one imagines the experience of the smoke-like apparition [see p. 87]. One should meditate on this well and visualize the process clearly.

The next stage is the dissolving of the vowel sound u (Tib. zhabs.kyu) into the part of the letter above it. At this point, one should imagine that the fireflies-in-the-sky apparition has appeared [see p. 88].

Next, the *hā* merges into the head-line of the *hā*. At that time, one should imagine that there has appeared the apparition of the flaming butter-lamp [see p. 89].

Then, the head-line of the *hā* merges into the crescent moon disk. At this point, one should imagine that there appears the apparition of pale light [see p. 91, (1)].

Next, the crescent moon symbol merges into the drop. At this point, one should imagine there appearing the reddish light which is like the light of the sun [see p. 91, (2)]. The following stage is when the drop merges into the *nāda*. One should imagine that there appears the apparition of dense darkness [see p. 92, (3)].

One should then visualize the *nāda* dissolving into emptiness and imagine that there occurs the appearance of an extremely clear sky, like the sky at dawn that is unpolluted or untainted by anything whatsoever [see p. 92, (4)].

At this point, one should cultivate the pride, identifying with one's own resultant Dharmakāya. In this experience, there should be three qualities:

1) the appearance: clear emptiness (Tib. stong.gsal);
2) what one ascertains: the lack of inherent existence;
3) the experience: the experience is of the nature of great bliss. And this is speaking of the experience of the mind. At this point, the nature of the mind is the nature of the great bliss - the mind is experiencing great bliss.

In this way, one is following a sequence of meditation which parallels the death process.

Engaging in and becoming accustomed to this meditation practice as described acts as a means to free one of fear at death. If one has an authentic and fully qualified practice of this meditation, then one gradually develops and reaches the culmination of the stage of generation and goes on to the stage of completion.

There is also the practice of 'taking the Truth Body as the path' in the stage of completion, where it is by means of the 'facsimile of the clear light and the actual clear light' (Tib. dpe. dang.don. gyi.'od.gsal) that the basis, which is ordinary death, is purified. Briefly, what is referred to as 'facsimile of the clear light' is the mind which realizes emptiness, but in which the realization is mixed with a conceptual generic image. On the other hand, 'the actual clear light' refers to the mind which directly, non-conceptually realizes emptiness. To sum up, in both the stage of generation and the stage of completion, the basis to be purified is ordinary death.

If one attains the facsimile of the clear light in the stage of completion, one will experience no ordinary death at all; one will be freed of ordinary death altogether. But that is a very difficult attainment. It is not so likely that we will attain it in this life. But simply following this practice, whether or not one attains this very high realization, does act as a means to dispel the fear at death. And our own death is something which we can be entirely certain will come. However, by engaging in this practice, in which there is a parallel to the phases of the death process, we can become accustomed to it. By being accustomed to it, when eventually the actual death comes and when one experiences it, then one can pass throught it without fear. Since one knows what to expect, one has become accustomed to it. This can be likened to the people who jump from tremendously high rocks or cliffs into the water many floors down and sometimes do fantastic somersaults as they go. Just watching them for the first time, one might think that it would be terrifying to do that. Nevertheless, they become accustomed to it and then the fear is gone.

Here is another example: if you have never flown in an airplane, the first time up might be pretty scary; but if you have flown in them a lot, then it is 'old hat.' There is no fear at all because you have become accustomed to it.

Likewise, here in the meditation, one is going through a kind of rehearsal for the death process and becoming accustomed to it. Then instead of having fear when passing through the actual death process, previous habituation with the meditation will cause one to think of one's spiritual mentor and one's meditational deity. If one has these in mind at death, it is certain that one will not take a rebirth in the lower realms of existence in the immediately following life.

A very famous Tibetan lama, Longdol Rinpoche said, "In the morning, through my spiritual practice as a gelong, a monk, I cultivate the causes for having a divine rebirth. In the evening, I cultivate causes for taking a divine rebirth. And so, I am delighted with death. I am happy to die." This same lama did take birth as one of the lineage-holder kings of Shambhala.

This point about the morning and evening especially indicates the great potency of tantric practice. For example, in the morning, if one is carrying the imprints of having committed one of the tantric root downfalls and one dies, one will definitely go to a vajra hell. Whereas, if one does not die in the morning and receives empowerment or does self-empowerment, one can purify that. Then if one were to die in the afternoon, one could take an extremely fine rebirth. This indicates the tremendous power of tantra.

The Seventh Dalai Lama, Kelsang Gyatso, said that if through the practice of spirituality, that is, engaging in wholesome actions, one can die with delight, die with joy, then by all means, one should practice the Dharma.

As the Kadampa geshes of old used to say, "If one has Dharma, there is no fear of death. Why would there be any fear of death?" Surely this is so - if one has a strong spiritual practice, specifically this practice here, there would be no fear at death. One would simply see that one is discarding this old body and getting a new one instead.

We have gathered here out of devotion to Dharma, turning our minds to it. This is an extremely good and faultless choice because, especially at the point of death, there is nothing apart from Dharma that will be of the slightest benefit. Teachings from a lama or from the Buddha need not be accepted with blind faith. We can check up on these and, really giving them some profound thought, reflect, "When the time of my own death comes, what will be of benefit? If I have a hundred houses, a hundred automobiles, a thousand airplanes, no matter what kind of things I have accumulated, of what benefit will these be to me at the time of death? Even my own body, which has been created simultaneously with me in my mother's womb and which I have had for the duration of my life and have given so much attention to (providing it with clothes, food and medicine) and which has been an object of great cherishing, will have to be discarded . . . . It goes without saying that the other things that I have accumulated will also have to be discarded." At the point of death, only spiritual practice is of true and real benefit.

NOTES

[1]Dr. Yeshi Dönden, *The Ambrosia Heart Tantra*, translated by Ven. Jhampa Kelsang Dharamsala, Library of Tibetan Works and Archives, 1977), p. 13: "The six proper attitudes are:
1. thinking of oneself as being like an ill person.
2. thinking of the teachings as being the medicine.
3. thinking of one's teacher as being the doctor.
4. regarding all the Awakened Ones as supreme beings and thus sound sources of knowledge.
5. wishing for the flourishing of the teachings.
6. having the intention to overcome one's personal faults by practicing the teachings."

[2]Lati Rinbochay and Jeffrey Hopkins, *Death, Intermediate State and Rebirth in Tibetan Buddhism* (Valois, New York: Gabriel Press, 1979), pp. 38 and 42: "After the four elements dissolve, the five phenomena on the level of the aggregate of consciousness must dawn in stages. These five are the mind of eighty indicative conceptions, the mind of radiant white appearance, the mind of radiant red increase, the mind of radiant black near-attainment, and the mind of the clear light of death . . . . The sign of the mind of appearance itself - when those eighty indicative conceptions have dissolved into it - is the dawning of extreme clarity and vacuity as well as of light with a white aspect like a night sky pervaded by moonlight in the autumn when the sky is free of defilement."

[3]*Ibid.*, p. 42: "It is called 'appearance' [because an appearance like moonlight dawns][30] and 'the empty' [because of being devoid of eighty conceptions as well as the wind that serves as their mount]."

[4]*Ibid.*, p. 43: "It is called 'increase of appearance' [because of being very vivid like sunlight][31] and 'the very-empty' [because of being devoid of the mind of appearance as well as the wind that serves as its mount]."

[5]One encounters a great deal of discussion about the 'cone of the psychic heat' and obviously, there is a great deal of meditation which is done about this point relating to the red bodhicitia at the navel.

[6]*Ibid.*, p. 44: "It is called 'near-attainment' [because of being near the clear light][32] and the 'great-empty' [because of being devoid of the mind of increase as well as the wind that serves as its mount]."

[7]*Ibid.*, p. 46: ". . . just as space is a vacuity that is a mere negation of coarse obstructive contact, so appearances of coarse conceptuality have disappeared for those minds and an appearance of vacuity dawns during the four 'empties' [empty, very-empty, great-empty and all-empty] . . . . The modes of appearance [in these four states] are similar to an autumn sky, and so it is used as the example. It is not that appearances of the sky and so forth dawn on these occasions."

[8]*Ibid.*, p. 45: "This is called the 'clear light of death' and 'the all-empty' [because of being devoid of eighty conceptions, and of appearance, increase and near-attainment as well as of the winds that serve as their mounts]. It is actual death."

[9]There are the 'subjective' and the 'objective clear light':
The subjective clear light Tib. yul.can.gyi. 'od. gsal) is the mind realizing emptiness.
The objective clear light (Tib. yul.gyi. 'od.gsal) is emptiness itself.

SECTION SEVEN

As we receive these teachings, we should dispel the ordinary appearance and conceptualization of this place by imagining it to be the palace of Kālacakra. Furthermore, the ordinary appearance and conceptualization of onself [and others] should be dispelled by generating oneself as Kālacakra with one face and two arms. The Guru should also be conceived of as Kālacakra. Then, listen to these teachings with a motivation aspiring towards the highest enlightenment for the benefit of all living beings.

[III. A.]

2. TAKING THE ENJOYMENT BODY OF THE BUDDHA AS THE PATH IN CONJUNCTION WITH THE ORDINARY INTERMEDIATE STATE

It is very important to know that in the Kālacakra Tantra, there is no practice of taking the Enjoyment Body (Skt. sambhogakāya; Tib. longs.sku) as the path with regard to the intermediate state. The reason for this is that if one purifies the ordinary death and the ordinary birth, by the very force of that, one naturally purifies the ordinary intermediate state. Consequently, a separate practice is not necessary. In the Kālacakra Tantra and its teachings, there are a number of uncommon points which differ from other tantra teachings such as those found in the Vajrabhairava, Guhyasamāja, Cakrasaṃvara and Hevajra, where there is the possibility of attaining enlightenment during the intermediate period, as well as during this life or a subsequent life. In these tantras, there is the practice of taking the Sambhogakāya as the path in relation to the intermediate state, whereas in the Kālacakra, one either attains full enlightenment in this lifetime or in a lifetime thereafter, but not during the intermediate period.

To understand this aspect of meditation, [taking the Enjoyment Body of the Buddha as the path in conjunction with the intermediate state,] it is necessary to know the process of the intermediate period. [And to understand better this process, let us look at some parallels first.]

When we fall asleep in our present state and consciousness gradually dissolves or recedes, the following very subtle signs occur: a mirage-like sign, a smoke-like sign, a sign similar to sparks or fireflies, and sign like a still candle flame. After these signs have appeared, there occurs what is called the 'clear light of sleep' (Tib, gynid. kyi.'od.gsal). This is the name given to the dream consciousness which is only a mental consciousness, namely, it does not include any of the sensory consciousness. When the dream consciousness (Tib. gnyid.kyi.sems) manifests, one engages in various types of activities. During the dream period, one has a dream body with which one performs different activities.[1] Upon the conclusion of sleep, the energies converge at the heart like breath-mist on a mirror gradually drawing towards the center. One then awakens and engages in various types of activities.

This [entire process] is similar to the death state when one experiences the four signs and consciousness together with the energies converge at the heart. When the very subtle consciousness and the very subtle energy [that is, the forever indestructible drop] leave the body [through any of the nine orifices[2]], and the gross body made of flesh and bones is discarded, existence during the intermediate period begins. There is a parallel here.

THE INTERMEDIATE PERIOD

Birth as an intermediate being is called 'spontaneous' or, more literally, 'miraculous,' but it means spontaneous and sudden. With the sudden birth of one's body of the intermediate period (Skt. antarābhāva; Tib. bar.do), all of the five senses, the major and minor limbs (minor being the fingers, etc.) occur suddenly and simultaneously – unlike birth from a womb in which the senses and the limbs are formed very gradually. Such a being is called a 'smell-eater' (Tib. dri.sa) because it feeds on smells. It is also called 'the one searching for rebirth.'

100

During this period, one's body is composed only of consciousness (Tib. sems) and energy (Tib. rlung), and it is very, very subtle. Wherever one's thoughts are directed the body spontaneously goes there – one thinks of a place and the body is immediately there. It moves effortlessly, just by the direction or application of the mind to a certain place.

Intermediate existence is a very strange kind of existence. Except for the mother's womb into which one will eventually enter, one's body is unobstructed by anything solid, such as buildings or solid structures. The second quality is that by the force of karma, one has certain supernormal powers. Thirdly, one has a degree of natural clairvoyance or heightened awareness.

The intermediate being (and the intermediate existence itself) is called the 'foundation Sambhogakāya' (Tib. gzhi'i.longs.sku). Keep the word 'foundation' clearly in mind as referring to the present time. In addition to the foundation Sambhogakāya, there are the 'path Sambhogakāya' and the 'ultimate Sambhogakāya.' The foundation and the path Sambhogakāyas are not the actual Sambhogakāyas; only the ultimate one is the actual Sambhogakāya. The others are merely given the above names as designations.

To understand why this body of the intermediate existence is called the foundation Sambhogakāya, one needs to look at the nature of the actual Sambhogakāya of a Buddha. The actual Sambhogakāya is not made up of gross matter such as flesh and blood, but is simply composed of consciousness and energy. This is a subtle body that is adorned with major and minor marks of a Buddha. Similarly, the composition of a body during the intermediate period is also that of consciousness and energy, and is very subtle. It is because of this parallel that the body of the intermediate existence is called the 'foundation Sambhogakāya.'

The point of the meditation with regard to the foundation Sambhogakāya is to purify the ordinary intermediate period which comes through the force of mental distortions and actions motivated by mental distortions. During the path Sambhogakāya, one is creating causes for the arisal of the actual Sambhogakāya. Finally, there arises the Sambhogakāya at the time of the result, which is actual, ultimate Sambhogakāya, the culmination of one's spiritual practice.

If one meditates now on the stage of the practice which takes the Enjoyment Body as the path in conjunction with the intermediate period this acts to dispel many fears that would normally occur during the intermediate state period.

3. TAKING THE MANIFESTATION BODY OF THE BUDDHA AS THE PATH IN CONJUNCTION WITH ORDINARY BIRTH

The Enjoyment Body of a Buddha has such a subtle form that it is only accessible to the Mahāyāna Ārya Beings. In order to benefit and be accessible to a greater number of beings directly, the Enjoyment Body manifests in the grosser Manifestation Body (Skt. nirmānakāya; Tib. sprul.sku). The parallel to this [transformation of the Sambhogakāya into the Nirmānakāya] is that of the intermediate being entering the combined regenerative substances of the parents and taking birth.

In order to discuss 'taking the Manifestation Body as the path in conjunction with birth,' first of all, it is necessary to understand the nature of conception and the birth process. If one understands this well, one can realize the truth of former lives. There is no doubt whatsoever concerning the certainty of former and latter births. If future lives did not exist, Dharma practice would be irrelevant. If Dharma practice were irrelevant, we could simply put the energies of this life into having the best of times knowing that at death everything would be finished. However, a very clear understanding of the process and the nature of conception and birth beings to light conclusive evidence indicative of former and latter lives.

a. CONCEPTION

The following teaching comes from the sūtras, specifically the *Sūtra on Entering the Womb* (Tib. mngal.'jug.gi.mdo). For consciousness to enter into the womb and for conception to occur, there must be three conducive factors, as well as the absence of three faults:

The first of these three conducive or vital factors is that there be no disorder of the womb of the mother and that she does have the menstrual cycle.

The second vital factor is that the intermediate being must be nearby and accessible so as to be able to enter. It should be very clear that there must be an intermediate being in the proximity of the future parents for the conception to take place.

The third conducive factor is that male and female have sexual intercourse.

The first of three faults that must be missing for conception to occur is that there must be no defect in the womb of the mother. Due to an imbalance in the so-called three 'humors' of wind, bile and phlegm, or through some other disorder ["the mother's womb must be free from the fault of its center being like the shape of a barley seed, an ant's waist or a camel's mouth"], it is possible for a blockage of the womb to occur so that conception cannot take place.

The second fault that must not occur is that the regenerative fluids of either the male or the female do not descend; the regenerative fluids of either the male or female must not fall at different times, that is, one early and one late; even if they do descend simultaneously, the male's [as well as the female's] regenerative fluids must not be 'rotten' or lack potency.

The third fault is the fault of karma: the karma on the part of the intermediate being to have these two people as parents must not be missing. And likewise from the parents' side, their karma for having this intermediate being as their child must not be missing.

To sum up, the three conductive factors are: freedom from the three faults; the intermediate being must be in proximity; the male and female must have sexual intercourse. If any of these are missing, conception cannot take place. The three faults are: the fault of the womb; the fault of the seed; the fault of karma. If any of these faults are present, conception cannot take place.

At the time its future parents are engaged in sexual intercourse, the intermediate beings sees only their sexual organs, but in the manner of a mirage, an illusory type of image or vision. Concurrent with this sight, the being's own desires arise. If this being is to be a female child, there is desire/attachment for the father and aversion towards the mother. If it is to be a male child, there is desire/attachment for the mother and aversion for the father. [However, ". . . . when the intermediate being begins to embrace the one that is desired, through the force of previous actions it does not perceive any part of the body except the person's sexual organ, whereby anger is generated."[4]. This anger and "desire . . . act as the cause of death . . ."[5], bringing the intermediate period to an end, [i.e., the intermediate being dies,] and consciousness enters the womb.

During intercourse, the movement of the sexual organs causes the 'downward-dispelling' wind to move and become agitated, and an ordinary 'psychic heat,' which is not an actual tum.mo, arises. Due to that, the boḍhicitta melts and descends. Eventually, thick regenerative fluids arise. ["After that, these drops of semen and blood, which definitely do emerge from both male and female . . . "[6]] descend and mix [in the mother's womb], forming a viscous mixture, like skim on top of boiled milk. It is at that point that consciousness enters the mixture in the mother's womb[7], and the fetus begins to grow.

b. FORMATION OF THE SEVENTY-TWO THOUSAND CHANNELS

There are 72,000 channels (Skt. nāḍī; Tib. rtsa) in the body that gradually begin to form at the heart during the gestation period in the womb. The principal one, which runs like a central shaft in the body, is called the 'central channel,' the uma (Skt. avadhūti; Tib. dbu.ma). The channel on the right is called the roma (Skt. rasanā; Tib. ro.ma) and the channel on the left, kyangma (Skt. lalanā; Tib. rkyang.ma). These form at the heart while [the fetus is still] in the womb.

The other channels that initially form at the heart are the sumkorma (Tib. sum.skor.ma) channel to the east (front), the döma (Tib. 'dod.ma) channel to the south (right), the düdrälma (Tib. bdud.bral.ma) channel which is immediately next to the central channel (a very bad channel because it constricts the other channels and prevents the energy from flowing freely), the khyima (Tib. khyim.ma) channel to the west (back), and the tum.mo (Tib. gtum.mo) to the north (left).

Initially, five channels form simultaneously: uma, roma and

kyangma, as well as the sumkorma of the east and the doma of the south. After that, the düdrälma, the khyima and the tum.mo channels occur simultaneously. These are called the eight initial channels at the heart.

The channels in the four [cardinal] directions divide into the four channels of the intermediate directions: the southwest, northeast, and so forth. Thus, there are the initial four and the intermediate four, which makes eight. Each of these develops a three-fold branch, which makes 24 branches. If one goes into more advanced stages of meditation on the body-mandala practice, one uses these 24 in the meditation.[8] These 24 similarly branch into three, making 72. Each of the 72 channels divides into a thousand, making 72,000.

This is the manner in which channels are formed during the gestation period. If you remember 24, you will be doing quite well. Even if you cannot remember 24, please do not forget the three central ones: uma, roma and kyangma. These you must remember!

c. FORMATION OF THE PRINCIPAL AND SECONDARY ENERGIES

One should know that the 'energies' or 'wind-energies' (Skt. vāyu; Tib. rlung) are at the root of both samsāra and nirvāna. It is by way of the energies that one goes either to liberation and full enlightenment or to the lower realms of existence. Apprehension of any type of object, for example, is made in conjunction with the energies. Mental distortions such as attachment and anger also arise in conjunction with energies. The energies and states of consciousness are very intimately related.

In other tantras such as Vajrabhairava, Guhyasamāja, Cakra-samvara, there are descriptions of the 'five principal energies' and the 'five secondary energies,' making ten [altogether]. In the Kālacakra Tantra, this particular terminology is not used, but there is still an explanation of ten energies.

1) In the explanation of the manner of the formation of energies, one initially speaks of what is called the 'life-sustaining energy' (Skt. prāna-vāyu; Tib. srog.'szin.gyi.r-lung). This energy is of two degrees: the subtle (Tib.

phra.mo) and gross (Tib.rags.pa). During the death process, the various energies gradually dissolved into the subtle life-sustaining energy.[9] It is the gross life-sustaining energy that maintains the relationship and acts as the link between the body and the mind – it sustains one's life.

[In the death process,] the gross life-sustaining energy having already dissolved,[10] there remains only the subtle life-sustaining energy[11] during the experience of the clear light [of death]. This subtle energy is always with us, inseparable [from us], and it goes to the next life.

During the first month following conception, the subtle life-sustaining energy gives off a gross life-sustaining energy. At this time, the shape of the fetus is like a fish.

2) In the second month, there occurs the 'downward-clearing energy' (Skt. apāna; Tib. rlung.thur.sel). The shape of the fetus is like a turtle, insofar as it really does not have any distinct features except a little lump for the head and little lumps starting to protrude for the limbs.

3) The energy that occurs during the third month, when the fetus is in the shape of a wild pig, is called the 'fire-accompanying energy' (Skt. samāna; Tib. rlung.me.mnyam).

4) During the fourth month, there arises the 'upward-moving energy' (Skt. udāna; Tib. rlung.gyen.rgyu). At this time, the upper part of the fetus' torso is larger, taking on a shape somewhat similar to that of a lion.

5) During the fifth month, the 'pervasive energy' (Skt. vyāna; Tib. khyab.byed.gyi.rlung) arises. The shape of the fetus, at this time, is like a very short person, definitely a human shape, but very short.

6) During the sixth month, there arises an energy which is specifically related to the visual faculty, the eye organ, called the 'moving energy' (Tib. rgyu.ba). At this time, the earth element arises.

7) During the seventh month, there arises another energy, which is specifically related to the auditory faculty, the ear organ, called the 'fully moving energy' (Tib. rnam. par.r-gyu.ba). At this time, the water element arises.

8) During the eighth month, there arises the 'perfectly moving

energy' (Tib. yang.dag.par.rgyu.ba) associated with the olfactory faculty. The fire element arises at this time.

9) During the ninth nonth, there occurs the 'very moving energy' (Tib. rab.tu.rgyu.ba). This is associated with the gustatory faculty (tongue) and the wind element.

10) During the tenth month, there occurs the 'certainly moving energy' (Tib. nges.par.rgyu.ba), associated with the tactile faculty, the organ of touch or tactile feeling. With this arises the element of space. This is not to say that the fetus takes ten months for gestation. According to the Buddhist tradition of Tibet, gestation takes nine months and ten days; so it would be following the ninth into the tenth month.

The is the manner of the arisal of the various energies and how they gradually manifest during gestation in the womb. However, none of them passes through the nostrils while one is still in the womb. It is only after birth (from the womb) that these energies begin to circulate and actual breathing occurs. The birth with this ordinary body is called the foundation Nirmāṇakāya (Tib.gzhi'i.s-prul.sku.) The way that the foundation Nirmāṇakāya relates to conception, gestation and birth, namely, the formation of the body, must be known in order to fully understand and practice the stage of generation.

d. FORMATION OF THE DROPS

To understand the nature of the formation of the drops (Skt. bindu; Tib. thig.le), one should remember the explanation about the indestructible drop at the heart [see p. 91]. There is the white bodhicitta (Tib. thig.le.dkar.po) of the father and the red bodhicitta (Tib. thig.le.dmar.po) of the mother. Both of these drops combine at the heart, so that the white bodhicitta is on the top and the red bodhicitta is on the bottom, forming the indestructible drop (Tib. mi.shigs.pa'i.thig.le). It is about the size of a sesame seed and is mixed with the 'extremely subtle consciousness' and the 'extremely subtle energy.'

During the period of gestation, a part of the white aspect [of the indestructible drop] at the heart ascends through the central channel, comes to rest and stays at the crown-center. This white bodhicitta at the crown-center is called 'Ham'. It is the source of the increase of the white bodhicitta throughout the body. A part of the red aspect of the indestructible drop at the heart descends to and remains at the navel-center. It is called the 'fire of psychic heat' (Skt. caṇḍālī; Tib. gtum.mo). This red drop at the navel directly increases the red element throughout the body.

In all of the 'energy-centers' or cakras, there are portions of these drops, but the chief place of the expansion of the white element/bodhicitta is the 'crown-center of the great bliss' (Tib. spyi.bo.bde.chen. gyi.'khor.lo), and the main place of the increase of the red element/bodhicitta is situated at the navel ['emanation-center' (Tib. sprul.pa'i.khor.lo)]. The indestructible drop at the 'heart [-center of Dharma' (Tib. chos.kyi.'khor.lo)], which is composed of both elements, increases both the red and the white bodhicittas equally.

e. ILLUSORY BODY

There are two types of 'illusory body' (Skt. Māyādeha; Tib. sgyu.lus): the impure and the pure.

The 'impure illusory body' is an illusory body in which one has not yet abandoned the obscurations to liberation (Skt. kleśāvaraṇa; Tib. nyon.mongs.pai'i.sgrib.pa) or, more literally, the obscurations of the mental disortions.

The 'pure illusory body' is the illusory body in which one has abandoned the obscurations to liberation.

Both of these illusory bodies are attained during the practice of this tantra. Ordinary people like ourselves would not be able to encounter or see an illusory body. It is something that is different from our gross body of flesh and bone, and arises separately. An advanced contemplative, who has reached that stage in the meditation, causes to arise the illusory body adorned with the major and minor marks of a Buddha. Such a being can go to various Pure Lands and there receive teachings, make offerings, and so forth.

Since this illusory body is neither accessible to nor encounterable by sentient beings, in order to be able to serve others, it merges back with the senses and into the gross body of the meditator. In that state, such a contemplative teaches the Dharma and serves in various ways. This is done during the stage of completion. Therefore, it is necessary to understand the process of conception and growth of the fetus, not only in relation to the stage of generation, but also to the stage of completion, so as to be able to attain the impure and pure illusory bodies.

The illusory body being out [of the body], its merging and returning back into the gross body, parallels the taking of a gross body at conception and the growth of the fetus.

MEDITATION PRACTICES OF TAKING THE THREE BODIES OF THE BUDDHA AS THE PATH IN CONJUNCTION WITH DEATH, INTERMEDIATE PERIOD AND BIRTH

One should see now very clearly the parallel of the three stages of death, intermediate state and birth: at death, there occur the dissolution of the various elements and the experience of clear light; this is followed by the intermediate period and then birth or conception.

The stages can be related to the following meditation practice:

a. In meditation, one successively dissolves the various elements, then experiences emptiness and identification with the Dharmakāya, having the three qualities which have already been stated.

b. Then, recognizing that as the Dharmakāya one is inaccessible to anyone but other Buddhas, there arises the motivation to manifest as the Sambhogakāya. In order for this to take place, there appears an eight-petalled lotus upon which rests a moon disc. Then the Dharmakāya, the Buddha-Mind itself, manifests as a blue pillar of light about one cubit long (from elbow to the tip of the middle finger). It is of the nature of the Buddha's Mind, and it represents the Sambhogakāya.

c. However, recognizing that as Sambhogakāya one is still inaccessible to many beings, one generates the motivation to manifest in a grosser form. In the process of transforming the Sambhogakāya into Nirmāṇakāya, this pillar of blue light (which is still standing on the eight-petalled lotus and moon disc) melts into the seat of the lotus and the moon, and oneself arises as Kālacakra, the Nirmāṇakāya. It is important to understand this parallel.

To sum up, in these meditation practices, the objects to be purified are the foundation [basic] death, intermediate state and birth. That which purifies those three, in that order, are: the taking of the Dharmakāya upon the path in conjunction with death; the Sambhogakāya in conjunction with the intermediate state; and the Nirmāṇakāya in conjunction with birth. These purifications are done by means of a practice which is of similar aspect to that which is being purified.[12] It is important to recognize this.

In other types of practices, one cultivates purifications which are contradictory to the object to be purified. For example, to dispel the misconception of grasping at a personal identity, a wisdom which is not in accordance with that ignorance, which sees through that ignorance, contradicts it and thereby dispels it, is cultivated and applied. Here, in the tantra, purification is not accomplished by a contradictory or incompatible antidote, but rather by the cultivation of an antidote which bears a similar aspect to that which is being purified. That which is purified and the purifier bear a similar aspect. So, upon purifying ordinary death, intermediate state and birth, one accomplishes the three Bodies of the Buddha.

The above three practices of taking the Dharmakāya as the path in conjunction with death, taking the Sambhogakāya as the path in conjunction with the intermediate state, and taking the Nirmāṇakāya as the path in conjunction with birth are the antidotes, the purifiers on the path of generation which act to suppress the ordinary death, intermediate period and birth. However, they do not completely eliminate these three ordinary events.

The actual remedy which truly and completely purifies and eliminates the death, intermediate state and birth occurs on the stage of completion through the 'facsimile clear light' and the 'actual clear light' [cf. p. 93].

The facsimile clear light (Tib. dpe.'od.gsal) is a conceptual realization of emptiness ('conceptual', meaning that the realization is mixed with a generic or conceptual image).

The actual clear light (Tib. don.gyi.'od.gsal) is a realization of

110

emptiness free from any conceptual image. It is a completely direct and non-conceptual realization.

To draw an example from the sūtra path, one engages in types of meditation on impermanence, suffering and so forth, which act to suppress or decrease the grasping, such as misconception with regard to the 'I.' However, these meditations do not actually dispel it, they simply suppress it. It is the wisdom that realizes identitilessness which actually dispels or eradicates that form of ignorance. So, there is a parallel here as well.

In order that this form of meditation may be practiced someday, the manner of the arising of the channels, the energies and the drops should be clearly understood. Furthermore, this understanding acts as the basis for the practice of the stage of completion; therefore, it is indispensable.

NOTES

[1]While one is dreaming, it is very important to recognize that one is in the dream state. Although this point is especially emphasized in the Kagyü tradition, it is, nevertheless, very important generally. If, while dreaming, one recognizes that one is dreaming, it is possible, while in the intermediate state, to recognize that one is in that state. By such recognition, much fear can be dispelled.

[2]Lati Rinbochay and Jeffrey Hopkins, pp. 53–4: "One who is to be reborn as a hell-being exits from the anus; as a hungry ghost, from the mouth; as an animal, from the urinary passage; as a human, from the eye; as a god of the desire realm, from the navel; as a *yaksha*, from the nose; as a god of magical accomplishment or as a 'probable-human', from the ear.[43] If one is to be reborn in the form realm, the exit is from the middle of the brow, and if one is to be reborn in the formless realm, it is from the crown of the head. These are set forth in the eighth chapter of *Samputa Tantra (Samputa)* and so forth."

[3]Lati Rinbochay and Jeffrey Hopkins, p. 58.

[4]*Ibid.*, p. 59.

[5]*Ibid.*

[6]*Ibid.*, pp. 50–60.

[7]*Ibid.*, p. 61: "...it should be understood that there are three doors of entry to the womb - the male's mouth, the top of the male's head and the door of the female's womb."

[8]This relates to the stage of completion, the advanced stage of this tantric meditation, which we must practice some day. There is another practice, on a whole different level, in which one meditates on the impurity or foulness of the body in order to dispel attachment for the body, because there is a natural conceit in thinking that one's body is so magnificent. That is a very good meditation.

[9]Lati Rinbochay and Jeffrey Hopkins, p. 15: "At the channel-centers there are white and red drops, upon which physical and mental health are based - white predominant at the top of the head, and red at the solar plexus. These drops have

their origin in a white and red drop at the 'heart', which is the size of a large mustard seed or small pea and has a white top and red bottom. It is called the indestructible drop, since it lasts until death. The very subtle life-bearing wind dwells inside it and, at death, all winds ultimately dissolve into it, whereupon the clear light of death dawns."

[10]*Ibid.*, p. 31: "At the time of death all the winds in the seventy-two thousand channels gather in the right and left channels. Then the winds in these two dissolve into the central channel. The winds in the upper and lower parts of the central channel finally dissolve into the indestructible life-bearing wind at the heart."

[11]*Ibid.*, p. 32: "The very subtle wind is the industructible life-bearing wind into which the final dissolution [in the death process] occurs. [Death occurs in this way] because, except for this very subtle wind, if the slightest wind that acts as a basis of consciousness dwells in any part of the body, death is not possible."

[12]Cf. The definition of the stage of generation, p. 83.

112

SECTION EIGHT

As always, we should begin by cultivating an awakening mind, aspiring for the highest, perfect enlightenment for the sake of all sentient beings. With this motivation, we should listen and practice these teachings in order to attain the enlightenment of Kālacakra and then bring all sentient beings to the same level of realization.

I encourage you to listen well and take notes as you desire, but not to leave it at that. After the class, you should read the notes again and again so that you can really become familiar with the material taught. There was a tradition of note-taking in Tibet as well. Patrul Rinpoche, a great Nyingma lama, pointed out the importance of not just taking the notes, rolling them up and putting them in the closet, but actually studying and making good use of them.

[III.]

B. CULTIVATING THE STAGE OF COMPLETION

Preliminary Teachings
1. FURTHER CHARACTERISTICS OF THE VAJRA BODY

As explained previously, in order to practice the stage of completion, it is indispendable to understand the way in which the channels, energies and drops arise. Within this presentation, one should, by all means, have a clear understanding of the three major channels: the central channel, uma, and on its right and left, the roma and kyangma, respectively.

In the explanation of the stage of completion there are three bodies: the gross, the subtle and the extremely subtle. Likewise, one can speak of the gross, the subtle and the extremely subtle minds. It is especially important to understand the nature of the very subtle mind because, nowadays, many people say, "There is no afterlife; there is only this one life." Such an assertion is founded upon the assumption that there is no subtle mind. It is true that the gross mind does not carry on after this life. But there is also the very subtle mind. If one really understands the very subtle mind and the very subtle energy, which is a very subtle form of the life-sustaining energy, and their functioning, then one sees that they have been with us since beginningless time and will carry on without end. By understanding them, one sees the logical basis for asserting both former and future lives. If future lives were not to exist, there would not really be any reason to practice Dharma at all. One could simply lead a hedonistic life.

A. The Energy-Centers

There are different presentations of the energy-centers (Skt.cakra; Tib. 'khor.lo). When one speaks of the four, they are:

1) the 'center of great bliss' (Skt. mahāsukha-cakra; Tib.b-de.chen.'khor. lo) situated at the crown of the head;

2) the 'center of enjoyment' (Skt. sambhoga-cakra; Tib. long-s.spyod.kyi.'khor.lo) at the throat;

3) the 'center of Dharma' (Skt. dharma-cakra; Tib. chos.kyi. 'khor.lo) at the heart;

4) the 'center of emanation' (Skt. nirmāṇa-cakra; Tib.sprul. pa'i.'khor.lo) at the navel.

When presenting five energy-centers, in addition to the above four, one speaks of:

5) the 'bliss-guarding center' (Tib. gsang.gnas.bde.skyong. 'khor.lo) which is located at the genital area.

Sometimes, there is also a presentation of the six energy centers.

1) The Center of Great Bliss

The center of great bliss at the crown of the head is situated in the area beneath the top of the skull and just above the brain. The width (of the center) is like a Japanese incense stick, about 1/8 of an inch or so. It is multi-colored: white, green, red and black. Its center is triangular in shape. At present, the central channel, uma, is constricted by two side channels, the roma and the kyangma, making a knot. These channels branch off into four and into eight, and so forth, eventually making a total of 32 subsidiary or branch channels branching off the center of great bliss. In appearance, this center resembles an open umbrella held aloft.

2) *The Center of Enjoyment*

This center is situated at the throat, right at the Adam's apple. Its color is red. The very center of the cakra is round. As above, the central channel is constricted by the two side channels, making a knot. The center of enjoyment has 16 branch channels, which branch out like an inverted umbrella. Clearly keep in mind that the previous center at the crown is like a right-side-up umbrella, whereas this throat-center resembles an inverted umbrella. Visualize them!

3) *The Center of Dharma*

The center of Dharma is situated at the heart, between the two breasts, in the chest. It is white in color. The center of this cakra is triangular in shape and is constricted three times, namely, there are three knots made by the two parallel side channels. It has only eight branch or subsidiary channels, which branch out like a right-side-up umbrella.
Think this over carefully. Get it clearly in mind so you can visualize it just as has been explained.

4) *The Center of Emanation*

This center is situated at the same height as the navel itself. Like the one on the crown, the emanation center is multicolored. Its center is round, while its 64 subsidiary channels branch out like an inverted umbrella.
So, the umbrella-like center at the navel are facing each other, just as the ones at the crown and the throat are facing each other.

5) *The Bliss-Guarding Center*

This center is situated at the genital area or, more precisely, at the very base or the very root of the genitals. Its center is triangular in shape and it is red in color. It has 32 subsidiary channels. The energy-center itself is like a right-side-up umbrella.[1]

One should understand that all of these centers are pierçed through the middle by the central channel, which acts as an axis for all them, as the trunk of a tree is the axis for its branches.

B. The Etymology of the Names of the Energy -Centers

It will also be helpful to understand why these five centers are called by their respective names:

1) Because the foundation of bliss, the white bodhicitta, abides principally at the crown, this center is called 'the center of great bliss.'

2) The enjoyment center at the throat is so called because this is the place where one tastes the six kinds of tastes: sour, sweet, bitter, salty, astringent and pungent.

3) The chief means, the chief instrument for the practice of Dharma is the mind, which has its main abode at the heart, specifically at the indestructible drop which comes from one's parents [see p. 107]. It is for this reason that the heart-center is called the 'center of Dharma.'

4) The basis of the emanation of great bliss is the fire of the psychic heat (Tib.gtum.mo'i.me), the tum.mo fire, the principal abode of which is situated at the navel. Therefore, this navel center is called the 'emanation center.'

5) The bliss-guarding center at the genitals is very closely related to the four types of joy [see p. 12] involving the movement of the bodhicitta in forward and reverse orders. Specifically, the spontaneous joy (Tib.lhan.skyes.kyi. dga-'.ba) is experienced when the bodhicitta reaches the very tip of the genital organ. Because it is so instrumental or critical to these various types of joy, this center is called the 'bliss-guarding center.'

It is important to understand well the etymology of the names of the five centers, as well as the previous explanation of the various types of energies or winds and drops, in order to use them in meditation. Remember especially the five principal energies: the life-sustaining energy, the downward-clearing energy, the fire-accompanying energy, the upward-moving energy, and the pervasive energy.

C. LOCATION OF THE FIVE PRINCIPAL AND FIVE SECONDARY ENERGIES

One should understand not only the manner of the arising of these energies, but also know their locations.

1) The life-sustaining energy abides at the heart and its function is to form the link between life (the vital force) and the body.

2) The downward-clearing energy is located at the genital area. Its function is to send downward and dispel, or retain and hold when necessary both the white and red bodhicitta, as well as urine and excrement. This type of energy can malfunction causing, for example, diarrhea.

3) The fire-accompanying energy abides at the navel. The word 'fire' here refers to the gastric fire. The function of the fire-accompanying energy is to separate the nutriment of one's food and drink from the waste (or the different stages of nutriment from the different stages of waste), sending the nutriment to sustain the various parts of the body and dividing the waste so that it goes into the various waste products.

4) The upward-moving energy abides at the throat. All of one's vocal activity, as well as swallowing food and drink, occurs by the functioning of this energy. In the death process, when this energy has dissolved, one is no longer able to speak or to swallow. One puts food or drink in the mouth and it just comes right back up again.

5) The pervasive energy pervades the entire body. Various physical movements of walking, leaning forward, leaning backward and so forth are all due to the functioning of the pervasive energy. When this energy declines, one loses the power of movement.

One should also consider the five secondary energies:

1) the moving energy resides at the eye and it apprehends form;

2) the fully-moving energy, which abides at the ear, apprehends sound;

3) the perfectly-moving energy, abiding at the nose, experiences odors;

4) the very-moving energy, which abides at the tongue, apprehends tastes;

5) the certainly-moving energy, which abides in the tactile faculty, apprehends objects of touch and different kinds of feelings or sensations.

A clear understanding of the different types of energies, channels and so forth is necessary for the meditations on the stage of completion which bring all of these various energies into the central channel and then into the indestructible drop at the heart. Unless the energies are first brought into the central channel, the realizations of the stage of completion are not attained. Whether one is meditating on the stage of completion or not, at death there occurs this retraction of the energies into the central channel and then into the heart. So, just as this naturally and effortlessly occurs in the death process, one is now duplicating it consciously in meditation.

Among the various types of the stage of completion and meditations, there are the 'vajra recitation' and 'vase-like meditation.' In the practice of these, the purpose is to draw the energies into the central channel and then to the indestructible drop at the heart.

D. THE FIVE PRINCIPAL AND THE FIVE SECONDARY ENERGIES AS RELATED TO THE FIVE BUDDHA FAMILIES

The five principal energies also correspond to the five types of Buddhas: the life-sustaining energy is the energy of Akṣobhya; the downward-clearing energy is that of Ratnasambhava; the fire-accompanying energy is the energy of Amoghasiddhi; the upward moving energy is the energy of Amitābha; and, finally, the pervasive energy is the energy of Vairocana.

The five secondary energies are also related to the five types of Buddhas: the moving energy is the energy of Vairocana; the fully-moving energy is the energy of Ratnasambhava;the perfectly-moving energy is the energy of Amitābha; the very moving energy is the energy of Amoghasiddhi; and the certainly-moving energy is the energy of Akṣobhya.

E. THE FIVE PRINCIPAL AND THE FIVE SECONDARY ENERGIES AS RELATED TO THE FIVE ELEMENTS

There is also a relationship between these energies and the various elements: the life-sustaining energy is related to the water element; the downward-clearing energy is related to the earth element; the fire-accompanying energy is related to the wind or the air[2] element; the upward-moving energy is related to the fire element; and the pervasive energy is related to the element of space.

Likewise, there is a relationship for the five secondary energies: the moving energy is related to the earth element; the fully-moving energy to the water element; the perfectly-moving energy to the fire element; the very-moving energy to the wind element; and the certainly-moving energy to the element of space.

F. The Energies and Their Respective Colors

There is also a distinction of colors with regard to these various energies: the life-sustaining energy is white; the downward-clearing energy, being related to the earth element, is yellow; the fire accompanying energy is dark green; the upward-moving energy, being related to the fire element, is red; and the pervasive energy is blue.

Likewise, these five colors are connected to the secondary energies: the moving energy is red; the fully-moving energy is blue; the perfectly-moving energy is yellow; the very-moving is white; and the certainly-moving is green.

G. The Ten Energies in the Kālacakra System

There is one vital point that has already been mentioned and which should be remembered. In general tantric presentations, there is the explanation of the five principal and five minor or secondary energies. The distinction in the Kālacakra is that the terminology of the 'five principal' and 'five secondary' energies is not used; nevertheless, the presentation of all ten is there [and the names of the first five energies are identical in both presentations].

1) The life-sustaining energy (Skt. prāṇavāyu; Tib.srog.'dzin.g-yi.rlung.);

2) the downward-clearing energy (Skt. apāna;Tib.rlung-.thur.sel);

3) the fire-accompanying energy (Skt. samāna; Tib.rlung-.me.mnyam);

4) the upward-moving energy (Skt.udāna;Tib.rlung.gyen.r-gyu);

119

5) the pervasive energy (Skt.vyāna;Tib.khyab.byed.gyi.rlung). The names of the next five energies are given in either Sanskṛt or English:

6) the nāga (Skt.nāga;Tib.klu) energy goes through the channel to the northwest;

7) the 'tortoise' (Skt.kūrma;Tib.rus.sbal) energy situated at the heart, flows through the southeast subsidiary channel;

8) the 'chameleon' (Skt. kṛkala; Tib. rtsangs.pa) energy flows through the southwest subsidiary channel and is of the nature of fire;

9) Devadatta (Skt. devadatta; Tib.lhas.byin) flows through the northeast and is of the nature of the water element;

10) Dhanañjaya (Skt. dhanañjaya; Tib.nor.las.rgyal) which, like nāga energy flows through the northwest, is of the nature of the earth element.

These are the names [as well as locations] of the ten energies in accordance with the exclusive tradition of the Kālacakra. There are some differences. Je Tsongkapa says the tradition of the Kālacakra is somewhat different from the other tantras, and he praises it very highly. It is stated that if one has a thorough understanding of the Kālacakra, then this understanding is easily applicable to understanding all the other tantras. It is a very important tantra.

There is an important point made in the context of the sūtras: it is stated that the root of the cycle of existence is the ignorance which misconceives of the self. In the context of tantra, it is stated that the energy is the root of both the cycle of existence and of liberation. In the detrimental aspect, there are the 80 conceptions, each of which is related to a corresponding type of energy. They keep us in the cycle of existence and cast us to lower states of existence. In this sense, the energy is acting as the root of the cycle of existence. Likewise, the energy is also at the root of enlightenment because there is an energy intimately related to, for example, the clear light. For each of the various mind states, as one progresses towards enlightenment, there are corresponding energies.

H. THE FOUR DROPS IN THE KĀLACAKRA SYSTEM

In accordance with the Kālacakra system, there are four types of drops (Skt.bindu;Tib.thig.le).

1) The 'drop of the arisal of deep sleep' (Tib.gnyid.'thug.skabs-.kyi.thig.le), which is chiefly energy, abides at the heart and at the tip of the genital organ.

When energies in the upper portion of the body, the head, the chest and so forth condense into the heart, and the energies in the lower part of the body condense into the genital region, one goes into deep sleep. The drop of the arisal of deep sleep is also called the 'mind-drop' (Tib.sems.sam.thugs.kyi.thig.le).

2) The 'drop of the arisal of dreams' (Tib. rmi.lam.skabs.kyi.thig.le) also abides at the genital region. When energies in the upper portion of the body converge at the throat, and the energies in the lower portion of the body converge at the genital region, one dreams. This is when the dream state occurs.

One often hears the statement that all phenomena are not truly existent and that they are like dreams. Take the case of a young woman who dreams she has given birth to a child whom she adores. She is enchanted by the child – she loves it so much. The child dies. She is incredibly distressed. She weeps and wails and goes through torment. Then she wakes up. There has not been any child, there has not been any death of the child, and she is out of that suffering. Likewise, for conventional truth, although phenomena do not truly exist, nevertheless, the relationship between actions and their results, that is to say, the law of karma, of suffering and of happiness, conventionally do exist. This drop of the arisal of dreams is also called the 'speech-drop' (Tib.ngag.gam.gsung.gi.thig.le).

3)The 'drop of awakening' (Tib.sad.pa'i.skabs.kyi.thig.le) abides chiefly at the forehead and the navel. When energies in the upper portion of the body converge at the forehead and the energies in the lower portion of the body converge at the navel, one awakens from sleep. This is what happens each morning in Seattle around 7 or 8 o'clock. This drop of awakening is called "the body-drop' (Tib.lus.sam.sku'i.thig.le).

4) The 'drop of the fourth occasion' (Tib. bzhi.pa'i.gnas.skabs.

kyi.thig.le) abides at the crown of the head and at the genitals. The term 'the drop of the fourth occasion,' refers to the occasion of the sexual bliss that is experienced during sexual intercourse between a man and a woman. During that time, the energies in the upper portion of the body converge at the crown and the energies in the lower portion of the body converge at the genitals. Bliss is experienced with the descent of the bodhicitta. This drop of the fourth occasion is also called 'the drop of transcendental wisdom' (Tib.ye.shes.kyi.thig.le).

It is important to know these different drops because they are indicative of the type of practice that one follows in the deep sleep, the dream and the awakening states. Corresponding to each of these stages there is a practice that is to be followed.[3]

2. THE FOUR PRELIMINARY STEPS WITH SPECIAL EMPHASIS ON THE GURU YOGA

All of this is in preparation for the actual practice of the stage of completion. For this practice, one needs:

a. the proper teaching on refuge, namely, on how to avoid taking refuge in or relying upon false paths or upon extremist teachers (in other words, one must have a pure refuge);

b. the teaching on bodhicitta, which is superior to the paths of the Listeners (Skt.śrāvaka; Tib.nyan.thod) and the Solitary Victors (Skt. pratyekabuddha;Tib.rang.sangs.rgyas);

c. the teaching on Vajrasattva for the purification of unwholesome mental imprints and obscurations;

d. the teaching on guru yoga for swiftly receiving blessings.

Among these four subject headings, the one on guru yoga is especially important. The great Sakya Paṇḍita likened the blessing of the Buddhas to the rays of the sun. If one has some firewood, no matter how strongly the sun might be shining, the firewood does not burst into flame. One has to have a magnifying glass in order to ignite the actual flame. Likewise, even though the Buddhas are very powerful and are able to bestow great blessings, it is impossible to receive them without a guru. The guru and one's relationship to the guru are indispensable.

To further illustrate this, there is an account of the translator Marpa when he was living with his Guru Nāropa. One day Nāropa manifested the entire Hevajra Maṇḍala together with the deity. He then called out to his disciple Marpa, saying, "My son, Chökyi Lodro (which was Marpa's personal name), get up, rise up! Here is a vision of Hevajra!" He rose and was awestruck. Then Nāropa asked Marpa, "Which will you prostrate to? Will you prostrate to Hevajra or will you prostrate to me, your Guru?" Marpa thought, "Well, this is a very special event. Here is the yidam, the meditational deity himself, appearing. This is an extraordinary event. . . .I can always prostrate to my Guru, he is always here. I will prostrate to the yidam." And he did so.

Nāropa then responded with one verse, the essential meaning of which states that the yidams are an emanation of the guru. Having recited this stanza, he snapped his fingers and Hevajra, together with the entire maṇḍala, dissolved into his heart. Nāropa then told Marpa, "This was not properly done; you made a mistake! As a result of this, your personal (family) lineage will be short!" And, in fact, this was the case. Marpa had nine sons, but his hereditary lineage was cut. In contrast, for example, in the Sakya lineage, the hereditary lineage has been preserved right up to the present. Whereas in the Kagyü, although the Dharma lineage is very much preserved and is very much alive and flourishing, the hereditary lineage from Marpa ended long ago.

To continue that same story, Marpa found this very strange. He was very, very unhappy and worried about this because he found it so bizarre – "Why did I do that in that situation?" This must have been the ripening of a residue from a karma committed long ago. He had previously had many visions of Hevajra and he was devoting himself to the practice of the Guru as being superior to the Yidam Hevajra. He had no confusion on that point. Although he had this clarity, nevertheless, he acted in that way. He was very concerned and was wondering, "What is happening to me?" As a result of this inner consternation, he fell ill.

One day, Nāropa and Marpa went out to a pond to bathe. While they were there, a crow took a protection ring from Marpa and flew up in the air. Nāropa did a very special 'threatening mudrā' and shot down the crow. When the crow came fluttering down, he

123

took the protection ring and gave it back to Marpa saying, "Now you will be free from this problem, free from the māra." It was as if a māra had taken over his mind and influenced him. Then Marpa responded by asking what he should do? And he decided that he would simply like to meditate.

This threatening mudrā is a very powerful one when it is used by a highly accomplished person on the stage of completion. For example, such a practitioner could sit here, point this mudra at a far off fruit-tree, and he would be able to draw the fruit of that tree to himself. Then he could reverse the whole process and send the fruits back up to their respective branches. These supernatural things which one is able to do in the practice of tantra are a lot of fun. This is simply one of a number of feats that might be done.

The supernormal powers of the Buddhas and the Bodhisattvas are beyond the realm of conception of ordinary beings. The manner of the ripening of various actions and the relationships that occur in terms of the law of karma for ordinary beings, are equally astounding. For example, the bizarre physical deformities of some people born without a mouth, or those born with one leg that is enormous and the other one tiny, or one leg that is bent way backwards – in each and every case, there is a very profound karmic relationship which comes into play and which ordinary beings cannot comprehend.

To draw a practical parallel, take a nomad, for example, who is living way out in the wilds and has no contact with civilization at all, simply living all by himself. If such a nomad were told that there are things such as airplanes that fly through the air and they do not even flap their wings, or that there are trains and so forth, he would say, "That is nonsense, that is impossible! Of course, there are no such things!" He would never believe it. Likewise, when an ordinary person is told of some of the supernormal powers of the Bodhisattvas and the Buddhas they might seem totally unbelievable to him. Nevertheless, just as airplanes and other amazing technological feats have been created, likewise, these powers are facts. Just as one can be shown these inventions, the powers of the Bodhisattvas and Buddhas can also be shown. On another occasion, when Milarepa was leaving his Guru to go off into retreat to meditate, Marpa and his wife Dagmema came out to send him off. Marpa, as a farewell, cast off his ordinary form and appeared in the form of Cakrasaṃvara. That disappeared and he took the form of Hevajra. That disappeared and he took the form of Guhyasamāja. That disappeared and then he took the form of āli and kāli [vowels and consonants]. When this was done, he called out to Milarepa, saying,, "My son, have you seen?" Milarepa said, "Yes, I have. Yes, I believe. Might I also be able to accomplish such wonders as you!" Then he went off into retreat and, as is very well known, attained the same enlightenment as his Guru Marpa and was able to perform many supernormal feats, like flying in the sky and so forth.

With the same kind of reverence that Milarepa had for Marpa, so should one practice and look up to one's own guru.

There was also a girl, who was a disciple of a lama by the name of Sakya Gyeltsen. She practiced and was also able to perform the miraculous wonders of flying through the sky and do forth. In verses of praise, she also referred to the great Yogin Milarepa and his powers.

The previous Dagchen Rinpoche, Gongma Choglang Rinpoche, came to the province in Eastern Tibet, where there was a Sakya Monastery by the name of Langna Gompa, which literally means, "the Elephant-trunk Monastery." At that time, Rinpoche knew that there were going to be a lot of violent earthquakes in the area. He told the people around him, "If you want to be with me, then come into this room. If you don't want to, stay outside," and he gave them each a blessing cord. The earthquakes occurred then up to a point along a certain ridge of a mountain. They flattened a lot of houses, but no damage occurred to the house in which Rinpoche was living. Afterwards, he did pass away in that house. There were many devotees who wanted to bring his remains back to Sakya, but the people there told them, "No, this would not be correct, because Rinpoche had a definite reason for passing away here. So, his remains should be kept here." Then, they built a golden stūpa to hold the remains. This was adorned with a pearl parasol. It was a very precious and holy place. Many Tibetans suffering from various illnesses came there to circumambulate the golden stūpa and a great many of them were cured. It was considered a very holy site. Each year, this stūpa grew a little bit

THE FIVE PRINCIPAL AND THE FIVE SECONDARY ENERGIES (Tib. rlung)

		TATHAGATA FAMILY	LOCATION	ELEMENT	COLOR
FIVE PRINCIPAL ENERGIES					
1. Life-sustaining	srog. 'dzin. gyi.rlung	Akṣobhya	Heart	Water	White
2. Downward-clearing	rlung.thur.sel	Ratnasambhava	Genital area	Earth	Yellow
3. Fire-accompanying	rlung.me.mnyam	Amoghasiddhi	Navel	Wind	Dark Green
4. Upward-moving	rlung.gyen.rgyu	Amitābha	Throat	Fire	Red
5. Pervasive	kyab.byed kyi.rlung	Vairocana	Entire Body	Space	Blue
FIVE SECONDARY ENERGIES					
1. Moving	rgyu.ba	Vairocana	Eye	Earth	Red
2. Fully Moving	rnam.par.rgyu.ba	Ratnasambhava	Ear	Water	Blue
3. Perfectly Moving	yang.dag.par. rgyu.ba	Amitābha	Nose	Fire	Yellow
4. Very Moving	rab.tu.rgyu.ba	Amoghasiddhi	Tongue	Wind	White
5. Certainly Moving	nges.par.rgyu.ba	Akṣobhya	Skin Surface	Space	Green

larger. From that time forward, the inhabitants of the area say that there have never occurred earthquakes in that valley. In other places, when earthquakes do occur, the people naturally call out to Gongma Choglang Rinpoche, praying for his help. Such is the blessing that great lamas have.

Again, to paraphrase a stanza by Sakya Paṇḍita, who was himself an emanation of Mañjuśrī, "Merit accrued through service and devotion to the guru for the duration of just a fingersnap, outshines the merit that is accrued during a thousand eons of practicing the six perfections." This would include sacrificing one's own body, head, arms and so forth.

Therefore, with great delight and joy, one should engage in devotion and service to the guru. The people who are here at the center have the opportunity to devote themselves to their own guru in that fashion.

NOTES

[1]Gyalwa Gendun Drub, the First Dalai Lama, "To Entice the Minds of the Wise" (Notes on Kalachakra), in *Bridging the Sutras and Tantras*, trans. and comp. Glenn H. Mullin (Ithaca: Gabriel Press, 1982), p.13; "In the *Kalachakra Tantra*, the six pressure points, or 131 *chakras*, are as follows. The first is located just below the crown aperture of the skull and has four petals of energy channels. The second is at the forehead and has sixteen petals. The third is located at the throat and has thirty-two petals. The fourth, which has eight petals, is at the heart. The fifth has sixty-four and is located at the navel. The sixth has two branches: the first at the anus, with thirty-two petals, and the second at the centre of the jewel, with eight petals."

[2]The reader is reminded that the word 'air' or 'wind' (Skt. vāyu; Tib. rlung) is the same word that has been translated, in other instances, as 'energy.'

[3]Gyalwa Gendun Drub, the first Dalai Lama, pp. 135–6: "For ordinary beings the four drops carry the potency of inducing perception of the impure objects of the world, the potency of causing confused appearances and sound to arise, and the potencies giving rise to obscurity of mind, ignorance and perishable happiness. The aim of the Kalachakra yogas is to take these impure and obscured bases and to transform them into the path of enlightenment. To be specific, these three potencies are to be purified and transformed into the empty body, unconfused sound and unchanging bliss. These are cultivated to perfection, giving rise to the body, speech and mind of a Buddha and to ultimately pristine awareness."

SECTION NINE

It goes without saying that if we cultivate a very good motivation now, listen with this motivation, and then put the teachings into practice, this is extremely good. Even if we do not practice much, but simply have a good motivation while listening, very beneficial imprints are made upon our own mindstreams so that, in future existences, we will have propensities for gaining a very profound understanding of the Dharma.

In order to practice the stage of completion, one needs to understand the basis that one is working with. Prior to this, one should have at least the basic understanding of the stage of generation. There has already been an explanation of the channels and the various energy-centers, with the 32 branch channels at the crown of the head, the one with 16 at the throat, the one with eight at the heart, 64 at the navel and 32 in the genital region. One also needs to have the basic understanding of the three channels, the four principal energy-centers, the drops and the illusory body.

[III. B.]

MEDITATION PRACTICES ON THE STAGE OF COMPLETION

THE SIX BRANCHES OF THE PRACTICE

To go on to the stage of completion in the Kālacakra, one should know that there are 'six branches of the practice.' We have set for ourselves the goal of full enlightenment. To accomplish it, we should know what we are attaining: the Body, Speech and Mind of a Buddha. This is like the attainment of anything else. If we wish to go to India, we should first know the nature of our destination; if we are going to Tibet, we should know where we are headed.

Since we are headed for Buddhahood, it is the attainment of the Body, Speech and Mind of a Buddha which is required. The way to accomplish this goal is through the following the six branches of the practice.

1. The first of the six branches of the practice [or yoga of the Kālacakra] is called 'individual convergence' (Skt. pratyāhāra; Tib.sor.sdud). It is designed to draw together the individual energies of the five sensory consciousnesses into the heart.

As has already been explained, there is now a very intimate relationship between consciousness and energy. This can be understood in terms of an analogy. Imagine a person who has no legs but has clear sharp vision. Off in the distance, he sees a tree with fruit on it. He would like very much to eat that fruit, but having no legs he cannot get there. However, there is another person who is blind, but has both of his legs intact. He does not know where the fruit is, but he can walk around. If the two were to get together, the man with no legs riding on the shoulders of the man with legs but no eyes, then the man with the eyes could direct him, "Now go forward, then right, now left. . . ", directing the man with the legs to the fruit. Having arrived at the tree, he could pluck off the fruit and enjoy it. In like manner, the person with eyes is like consciousness; the person with legs is like energy. It is the consciousness that apprehends the object, but it is able to go to the object only by the force of the energy. It is the energy that enables the consciousness to come in contact with the perceived object. The two work together in that manner.

2. The second branch of the practice is called 'individual stability' (Skt. dhyāna; Tib. sor.gtan or bsam.gtan).

These two practices, the individual convergence and the individual stability, are the means of accomplishing the 'body of empty form' [see below, p. 131]. If this body has not been accomplished previously, it is accomplished freshly; and if it has already been accomplished, it is increased. These two act as a means for the attainment of the Body of a Buddha, the Nirmāṇakāya.

3. The third branch of the practice is called 'life-effort' (Skt. prāṇāyāma; Tib. srog.rtsol).[1] Its function is to draw the energy of the mental consciousness into the central channel. The energies of

129

the five sensory consciousnesses have already been drawn in by the previous practices.

The first syllable of this compound term, (Tib. srog), which literally means 'life' or 'life force', refers to the energy. The second syllable (Tib. rtsol) refers to the closing of the two side channels, the roma and the kyangma, and the drawing of the energies into the central channel. It implies the movement of the energies through the central channel. As long as these energies are flowing through the roma, the right side channel, there occurs hatred; and as long as the energies are flowing through the kyangma, the left side channel, there occurs attachment. To bring about the cessation of these two mental distortions, the active energies are not allowed to go through these side channels, but are drawn into the central channel.

4. The fourth branch of the practice is called 'retention' (Skt. dhāraṇā; Tib. 'dzin.pa). Its function is to retain the energy of the mental consciousness called the 'active ener ies of mental consciousness' (Tib. las.rlung) in the central channel.

Thus, it is through the life-effort practice that the active energies of mental consciousness are drawn into the central channel and, with the retention practice, they are retained there. Having done so, one achieves what is called 'mastery over the energies,' specifically the mastery over energies that are the root of speech. Hence, these practices act as a cause for attaining the Buddha's Speech, the Sambhogakāya.

There is a distinction between the sūtra and the tantra explanations of the Sambhogakāya. The sūtras explain the Sambhogakāya in terms of the five 'certain' or 'definite aspects,' whereas in the tantras, the Sambhogakāya refers to the Buddha's Speech.

5. The fifth branch is called 'recollection' (Skt. anusmṛti; Tib.rjes.dran). In this practice, the tum.mo, the fire of the psychic heat, flares up and melts the white bodhicitta, which [then] flows down to the tip of the genital organ (called the 'jewel') where it is retained (i.e., it is not allowed to come out) and, at this point, one experiences the spontaneous joy (Tib.lhan.skyes.kyi. dga'.ba). The recollection or the bringing to mind of this joy is what is involved in the fifth of these practices.

6. The sixth branch practice translates as 'concentration' or 'meditative equipoise' (Skt. samādhi; Tib. ting.nge.'dzin). It refers to the meditative equipoise of the non-dual bliss and emptiness. What is being referred to as 'bliss and emptiness' is as follows: the bodies of the deity and the consort are bodies of empty form called 'emptiness,' and the bliss is the supreme immutable bliss (Tib. mchog.tu.mi.'gyur. ba'i.bde.ba). Therefore, the attainment of the sixth practice is the meditative equipoise of the non-dual bliss and emptiness which, in this particular context, refer respectively to the supreme immutable bliss and the two bodies of the deity and the consort.

What is meant by the term, 'body of empty form'? In order to accomplish the body of empty form, one has to use up or exhaust the material element of one's body and then generate the form of the deity and the consort. Rather than being composed of [gross] matter, their bodies are composed simply of energy and consciousness. More specifically, they arise from the cultivation of the great bliss and the wisdom of emptiness. From these two aspects, there arise, in the divine embodiment of these two factors, the body, which is the body of empty form, and the mind of that body (colloquially called 'sem' and in polite speech referred to as 'thug'), which is the wisdom of the non-dual bliss and emptiness. Thus, it is this mind or this wisdom of the non-dual bliss and emptiness which is to be accomplished by these two final branch practices.

To draw a parallel in the world: a sprout needs to arise from a cause which is similar to itself – the seed. It cannot arise from a totally dissimilar cause. In like fashion, the result of this practice is the attainment of the body of the deity and the consort. To bring about this result, one needs to nurture or cultivate a similar cause, that is, a cause similar to that result.

[Here follows an explanation of the six branches of the practice in their reverse order:]

6. In order to accomplish the body of the deity and the consort, first there must be the attainment of the meditative equipoise of the union of the [non-dual] bliss and emptiness. This is what is involved in the concentration branch of the practice.

5. Prior to that, there has to be the attainment of the stage of the recollection practice.

131

4. For the stage of recollection to occur, there must be the previous attainment – the fourth of these branches of practices, 'retention.' With this practice, one unwaveringly retains the energies in the central channel, at the heart. Only when this is done is it possible for tum.mo fire to flame upwards and cause the white bodhicitta to melt and descend.

3. Before the stage of retention can be attained, there must be the prior accomplishment of the third branch of the practice, the life-effort. Without preventing the energies from passing through the two side channels and without drawing them into the central channel, it is quite obvious that one cannot retain them there.

2. & 1. In order to eventually draw these energies into the central channel, there have to be the initial two stages of this practice: the individual convergence and the individual stability. The purpose of these is to regulate the energies in order to make this process possible. Thus, the function of the first two branches of the practice is to make these energies fit for action, usable. If they are not made serviceable (Tib. las.su.rung.ba) through the training of meditation, it is not possible to bring them into the central channel.

The initial task of the first branch of the practice, the individual convergence, is designed to draw the active energies associated with the five sensory consciousnesses into the central channel. Only when this is accomplished is it possible to draw the energies into the central channel and prevent them from passing through the side ones. All of this must be done in sequence.

There are 11 signs of having brought the energies of the five sensory consciousnesses into the central channel and they will be explained later. Also, in this process (of bringing the energies into the central channel), there are three major stages:

● 'Entering' (Skt. praveśa; Tib. 'jug). The sign of the energies entering into the central channel is that the force of the breath through both nostrils is even in strength. Normally, the breath is stronger through the left or the right nostril.

● 'Abiding' (Skt. ālaya; Tib. gnas). The sign of the energies abiding in the central channel is that the flow of the breath through both nostrils ceases entirely and there is no further movement of the abdomen, that is, respiration has stopped.

• 'Dissolving' (Skt. utthāna, thim). The signs of dissolving the energies into the central channel include the sequence of signs beginning with the smoke-like apparition through to the clear light. These signs, which have been explained previously appear in their respective order.

The following is a very concise explanation of the six branches of the practice [in their original order].

1. & 2. The first two, ·the individual convergence and the individual stability, are designed to accomplish the Buddha's Body. They train and regulate the energies in order to draw them into the central channel.

3. The life-effort practice is designed to prevent the energies [of mental consciousness] from passing through the two side channels and to draw them into the central channel.

4. The retention practice is designed to retain those energies that have been drawn into the central channel, not allowing them to waver in and out [of that channel].

5. On the basis of an already accomplished retention practice, one engages in the recollection practice, which involves the union with any of the three types of mudrās. This practice is designed to flare up the fire of the psychic heat which melts the bodhicitta. Its descent to the tip of the genitals is the cause for the experience of the spontaneous joy (Tib. lhan.skyes.kyi.dga'.ba).

6. That which is accomplished through the sixth branch of the practice, concentration, is the great union (Tib. bzung.'jugs). This is done through the attainment of the body of empty form of the deity and consort and [the experience of] the supreme immutable bliss (Tib. mchog.tu.mi.'gyur.ba'i.bde.ba) followed by the cultivation of their union. The result of practice is the attainment of the great union [cf. p. 14, 4].

There are two types of yogas known as the night and daytime yogas.

1. THE NIGHT YOGA

a. THE PLACE OF THE PRACTICE

The place in which one meditates during the practice of the night yoga should be dark. This has many benefits for the generation of the body of empty form. In the past, lamas who followed this practice were very meticulous about this point of sitting in a room which does not have even the tiniest glimmer of light. There was not even a crack the width of a hair in their rooms. It was totally dark. We might find such a practice impractical to follow for the time being; nevertheless, it is important to hear about it, as well as to have these mental imprints placed upon the mind.

b. THE POSTURE

During this meditation, one assumes a definite posture: the legs should be in the crossed-vajra position, with the left foot upon the right thigh and the right foot up on the left thigh. The hands should be in the mudrā of meditative equipoise: the left hand beneath the right with thumbs touching, palms facing upwards, and four-finger widths beneath the level of the navel.

An alternative mudrā is to put the thumb of each hand on [its respective] palms, make a clenched fist out of each and place them on the upper part of the thigh. This is particularly used for the practice of the individual convergence because of the emphasis on drawing the energies associated with the sensory consciousness into the central channel.

c. THE ACTUAL PRACTICE

There are a number of rather varying traditions concerning the actual mediation at this point. For example, one tradition instructs that one should direct the mind to the sky. Whereas, Gyeltsab Je states that this is ridiculous because the point of this practice is to draw the energies into the central channel. To bring the mind out, by directing it to the sky, would obviously not be of any benefit.

One begins the practice of this meditation by visualizing the central channel. Then, one should single-pointedly focus the mind upon the empty central channel, particularly at the point between the eye-brows in the forehead (Tib. smin. mtshams), which is also visualized as empty. As a related point and one that has previously been mentioned, mintsam is the place where the drops are situated at the time of awakening from sleep [see above, p. 121, 3)].

THE TEN SIGNS OF PROGRESS

If one engages in this practice properly, there will arise certain signs. There are four night and six daytime signs. The four night signs, which have already been explained and which occur as one draws the energies into the central channel, are:

1) the smoke-like sign
2) the mirage-like sign
3) the fireflies-like sign
4) the butter-lamp-flame-like sign.

The 'six signs that occur during the day are:

1) the sign of fire
2) the moon-like sign
3) the sun-like sign
4) the sign of Rāhu, which is like darkness or gloom
5) the sign 'of lightning
6) the blue drop.

If one meditates very well, this is how it happens.[2]

In the next stage, one visualizes a very, very tiny black drop in the central channel in the space between the eyebrows. Within that very tiny drop, one visualizes or imagines, as clearly as possible, the Sambhogakāya-like form of the Kālacakra embracing the consort and endowed with 'five certainties.' However, one must clearly understand that the appearance seen in one's field of imagination is not the actual Sambhogakāya because one is not able, at this point, to actually encounter the Sambhogakāya of a Buddha. Nevertheless, one visualizes or creates the deity with the consort in the Sambhogakāya-like form.

THE FIVE CERTAINTIES OF THE SAMBHOGAKĀYA-LIKE FORM

The first the five certainties is the 'certainty of time': after the appearance of the four signs of the night and the six signs of the daytime, the Sambhogakāya-like forms [of the deity and consort] are visualized and seen. In other words, the time of the Sambhogakāya-like form is the time after all of the ten signs have been experienced.

The second of the five certainties is the 'certainty of abode,' indicating that the deity and the consort appear in the central channel.

The third is the 'certainty of nature,' that is, the certainty that the deity and the consort are not composed of an aggregation of particles but are, rather, appearances of one's mind.

The fourth, the 'certainty of the body,' is the certainty of the appearance that occurs: the deity and the consort are Vajrasattva (Vajrasatta being the same as Vajradhara).

The fifth, the 'certainty of aspect,' is the certainty that the deity and the consort appear embraced in union. This is the form of the deities that should be seen within the central channel.

d. THE FUNCTION OF THE SIX BRANCHES OF THE PRACTICE

1) It is with the first of the six branches of the practice, the individual convergence, that one experiences the above-mentioned ten signs and then accomplishes the eleventh – the sign of the deity with the consort, as has been just explained. Thus, the function of the first branch is to accomplish [all of] the eleven signs.

2) The function of the second branch of the practice, the individual stability, is to stabilize that which has been accomplished by the first of the six branches.[3]

By means of the first two, individual convergence and individual stability, one makes these energies somewhat usable, fit for action and serviceable. As a result, the energies naturally begin to enter into the central channel.

3) It is at this point that one begins to practice the next branch, the life-effort. Keep in mind that this term is a very literal translation: 'life' (srog), in this context, refers to the energies, and 'effort' (rtsol) to the blocking of the two side channels (the roma and kyangma), as well as the drawing of the energies into the central channel (uma). It is after these energies have been made serviceable that one enters this stage of practice called the life-effort and engages in the two practices that have already been mentioned, the vajra recitation and the vase-like meditation [see above, p. 118].[4]

136

a) The Vajra Recitation

The task of practices of the stage of completion [as already mentioned several times], is to draw all of the ten energies into the central channel and then into the indestructible drop at the heart. To actualize this goal, there is an inner condition which is a type of meditation called the 'vajra recitation' (Skt. vajrajāpa; Tib. rdo.rje.zlas.pa). We have not heard about this kind of practice for many lifetimes.

By this tantric meditation alone, it is possible to bring into the heart four out of the five major energies: the life-sustaining, the downward-clearing, the fire-accompanying and the upward-moving energies, as well as the five secondary energies.[5] The fifth major energy, the pervasive is very difficult to draw into the heart. In order to do so, it is indispensable for the yogin to meditate in union with an actual consort or a ḍākinī (Skt. karma-mudrā). In other words, the real reason why [at a specific time] it is necessary for the yogin to actually engage in such a practice is to bring that final, pervasive energy into the heart.

For the vajra recitation, one should recognize the importance of the syllables Oṃ, Āh, Hūṃ. There is no mantra that is not included within this one mantra. It is the king of all mantras: the syllable Oṃ is the seed of the vajra-body; the Āh is the seed of the vajra-voice; the Hūṃ is the seed of the vajra-mind. In the actual practice, one visualizes the energy and the mantra as being inseparable, indivisible.

- As one inhales and the breath or energy comes in, one should imagine it to be the nature of the Oṃ, that is, as if the Oṃ is being drawn in together with the breath energy or the wind-energy.
- After inhaling, there follows [the phase of] the retention of the breath, which bears the syllable Hūṃ.
- The exhalation carries the syllable Āh.

This is a very short presentation of the vajra recitation, especially in accordance with the Kālacakra system,[6] and it differs somewhat from the Guhyasamāja presentation. It is very beneficial to hear about this tantric practice and to have such mental imprints, or simply to gain a brief understanding of it.

137

b. The Vase-Like Meditation

The purpose of the vase-like meditation is to draw together the life-sustaining and the downward-clearing energies into the heart-center. For an ordinary person, as the life-sustaining energy passes through the nostrils, there is a similar passage for the downward-clearing energy through the lower orifices. These two move together. However, in the vase-like meditation, one draws the two energies together (like two bowls joined together, facing each other) into and through the central channel, and then into the heart-center.

(1) Preparatory Practice

Right now, you should visualize the central channel (Skt. avadhūti; Tib. dbu.ma), which goes from the tip of the genitals through the center of the body like an axis. ["Its color is white on the outside and red within."][7] It is situated inside the body, a little more to the back than to the front. Furthermore, it goes right through the center, up through the throat, to the crown of the head, comes down and emerges right between the eyes. This is how you should visualize its upper end in meditation. You imagine the lower end going down just slightly below the navel.

The right channel (Skt. rasanā; Tib. ro.ma) is red in color [cf. p. 104]. Its upper end emerges from the right nostril and it runs about one finger width below the bottom tip of the central channel. This is an important point to remember.

The left channel (Skt. lalanā; Tib. rkyang.ma) is white in color and it emerges (at the upper end) from the left nostril, comes upward and then goes down next to and about one finger width lower than the bottom tip of the central channel.

Visualize these three as clearly as you can and, for a little while, meditate in this fashion.

Now, with your powers of visualization, take the right channel and insert it into the left channel, like placing one sleeve into another. This insertion of one channel into another is done just below the navel. Then, with the ring finger of your left hand, block the left nostril and inhale through the right nostril. Imagine, while you are doing so, that you are receiving the blessings of the guru, the Buddhas and all the Bodhisattvas. Inhaling in this fashion, imagine the blessings going through the right channel and, as they do so, purifying any faults of that right channel. The energy is then funneled into the left channel, following that little curve down by the navel. Having fully inhaled, retain the breath as long as possible, but exhale before any physical discomfort sets in. Do not really strain yourself by any means. If you retain the breath for too long to the point of feeling really uncomfortable, rather than helping you, this will simply harm your health. So, again, hold the breath just as long as you comfortably can.

Then with the ring finger of your right hand, block the right nostril. Exhale through the left nostril while imagining that you are dispelling all anger and hatred [see above, p. 129, 3].

To reiterate: one inhales through the right nostril, draws the energy down through the roma and upon its entering the kyangma, one retains the breath or this energy in the kyangma (for as long as it is comfortable) and, finally, exhales through the left nostril. This process should be repeated three times.

Next, visualize the left channel as inserted into the right channel. Then, inhale through the left nostril. The energy passes through the kyangma and enters into the roma. Retain the breath in the right channel, the roma, for as long as possible, but only while it is still comfortable. As you inhale, you should imagine, just as before, receiving the blessings of the guru, the Buddhas and all of the Bodhisattvas. Then, exhale the energy that is coming up the right channel through the right nostril. As you do so, you should imagine all of your attachment and lust is being expelled. Inhaling through the left and exhaling through the right nostril should also be done three times.

For the third phase of this meditation, visualize that the tips of both the roma and kyangma are inserted into the bottom aperture of the central channel. You inhale through both nostrils; however, breathing should be free of the following three faults:

  • the fault of sound – you should be breathing so gently that you cannot hear the passage of the air;
  • the fault of breathing very forcefully;
  • the fault of breathing erratically–this is where the inhalation is longer than the exhalation or vice versa. It should be even.

As you are inhaling through both nostrils, you should imagine the breath-energy from the right nostril going through the right channel and, simultaneously, the breath-energy from the left nostril going into the left channel. The energy passes down through channels to the level below the navel, enters into the central channel and fills it. As was done previously while inhaling you imagine receiving the blessings of the guru and all the Buddhas and Bodhisattvas. Similarly, as before, retain the breath as long as possible. Then, exhaling through both nostrils, one imagines the energy coming through the central channel and being emitted through the point between the eye-brows, like a spotlight sending a ray of light up into the sky.

The inhalation through both nostrils, the retention of the breath and the exhalation through both nostrils are also done three times.

You should know that, in fact, due to the many constrictions of the central channel by the two side channels (the roma and the kyangma), no energy actually passes through the central channel [see above, p. 114, 1)]. If it were to pass through the central channel, there would be a very great force of virtue there but, for an ordinary person, it does not. It is by means of visualization that one imagines this happening.

(2) The Actual Practice

The first step in the vase-like meditation is to visualize oneself very clearly as Kālacakra.

There are two ways of practicing the vase-like meditation:one is to visualize the vase in relationship to the navel-center and the other way is to visualize the vase in relation to the heart-center. Both are correct; but the best way would be if one could practice with the vase placed at the heart. However, if a beginning practitioner engages in the vase-like meditation at the heart, instead of gaining realization, there is a great danger of actually disrupting the energies at the heart with a malfunctioning of the life-sustaining winds, possibly resulting in physical disorders. Therefore, it is more practical and less dangerous for the beginning practitioner to engage in this meditation by focusing at the navel-center [only]. By doing so, one avoids the above-mentioned dangers.

The next stage in this practice is to visualize the syllable Ham
at the navel-center. The syllable is of the nature of one's own
mind; it is the emanation of one's own mind.

The function of the vase-like meditation is to take energies from
the upper portion of the body and press them down, and to take
the energies from the lower portion of the body and draw them up.
It is like two bowls that join together like a vase.

In the actual meditation, one does this by drawing the energies
down from the upper portion of the body. This must be done very
gently, smoothly and slowly; otherwise, there is a danger of having
energy disorders in the upper part of the body, such as the
shoulders.

To draw up the lower energies, one closes the lower apertures.
Then, very gently, one draws these energies up to the navel.
Again, a strong emphasis: this must be done gently. For just as a
more forceful drawing down of the energies from the top can lead
to problems in the energy-flows in the upper portion of the body,
likewise, a too forceful or violent practice on the lower energies
can disrupt the energy-flows in the lower portion of the body in
such a way that one is no longer able to urinate or defecate
properly. It can mix up that whole system down there. Therefore,
it must be done gently.

Having drawn the energies together, the upper energies down
and the lower energies up, one then focuses them around the
navel-center and retains the breath as long as possible – again,
without discomfort.

Initially, one cannot retain the breath very long; therefore, one
engages in this practice for just a short time, then exhales.
Gradually, one's power of retaining the breath increases. Eventually, the various energies in the body will first enter into the
central channel, then abide there and, finally dissolve. Those are
the three stages of the practice [see above, pp. 132–3].

When you have attained that level, should you happen to fall ill
and experience physical discomfort, you can easily remove
yourself from it simply by going through this process [of entering,
abiding and dissolving energies in the central channel].

There was a Kadampa geshe, Geshe Gompawa, who was
meditating and during this vase-like meditation the various signs

appeared. So, of course, his respiration completely stopped. Seeing this, his disciples were very, very sad. They thought, "Oh, the lama has died!" and they started to weep and lament. Then, Geshe Gompawa came out of his meditation with a burst of laughter asking, "What's wrong with you?" And they said, "Well, we thought you were dead!" He responded, "No, I'd been feeling a little bit of physical discomfort. . . my body had not felt very good. So, I dissolved it!"

This was a brief explanation of the vase-like meditations, which are aspects of the stage of completion. It would be very good if one could cultivate this practice somewhat. However, until one has gained the authentic realization of the stage of generation, it is not possible to gain the actual realization of the stage of completion. Nevertheless, it is good to do it a little bit, because it places very beneficial imprints upon one's mindstream.

The purpose and the function of these [two] tantric meditations on the stage of completion is to draw the energies into and through the central channel and then into the heart-center. Once these energies have been drawn into the central channel, the function of the life-effort branch of the practice has been accomplished [see above, p. 136, 3)].

4) It is not the function of the third branch of the practice to make the energies firmly abide in the central channel. This is, rather, the purpose of the next stage of the practice called retention. After one has reached the stage where the energies are abiding firmly in the central channel, one is ready for the next stage.

5) The fifth branch of the practice is called recollection. These two stages need to be practiced for a long time. One does not practice one for just one day, going on to the next practice the following day. The nature of this fifth branch of the practice is the yoga of the psychic heat, the tum.mo yoga, which is designed to cause the flame or the fire of the tum.mo to rise up.

Once, when Gampopa came to Milarepa, Milarepa asked him what meditation practice he had been following and Gampopa described it. To this Milarepa commented, "Well, you don't get butter by squeezing a handful of sand. So, if you want to understand the nature of the mind, then you should follow my practice, the cone practice of the tum.mo yoga. By such means, you will realize the nature of the mind."

The result of this practice of causing the tum.mo fire to rise up is that the white bodhicitta at the crown of the head melts and descends through the central channel all the way to the point of the genitals, where it is retained. When one is highly advanced in the stage of completion, one never allows the white bodhicitta to be emitted [see p. 27, no. 5] but, as it descends to the very tip of the genitals, without (it) wavering, one retains it without any emission whatsoever. It is at this point that one experiences the initial moment of the immutable bliss (Tib.mi.'gyur.ba'i.bde.ba) and that the material components of the body and the various active energies (Tib.las.rlung) begin to be exhausted. This process has begun and it will continue as one proceeds in the later stages of meditation.

[6] By means of the first five branches of the practice, one accomplishes the sixth, called concentration. A more detailed explanation on the fifth and the sixth branches of the Kālacakra yoga is given on pp. 151–3.]

This presentation is the particular system of the Kālacakra that is different from the general Anuttara Yoga Tantra presentations, such as those found in the Vajrabhairava, Guhyasamāja, Cakrasaṃvara and Hevajra Tantras. In their practices, this body remains and, apart from this body, there arises the illusory body as Hevajra or whoever it might be. Then, one attains enlightenment as that particular illusory body, which arises separate and distinct from these present aggregates. In the Kālacakra system, on the other hand, this material body, together with the active energies, is gradually exhausted.

e. The Six Energy-Centers and the Process of Exhausting the Material Components of the Body, Active Energies and the Drops of the White and Red Bodhicitta Resulting in the Attainment of the Bodhisattva Grounds

As mentinoned before, it is the energies which are the root of saṃsāra and by extinguishing them, one extinguishes the root of karma. Also, as stated before, the consciousness itself is not able to contact an object; rather it is by means of its conjunction with the energies that consciousness is able to apprehend the object and relate to it [see above, p. 105, c].

To further understand the gradual process of exhausting the material components of one's body, and so forth, let us return to the energy-centers or cakras: the genital-center, the navel-center, the heart-center, the throat-center, the forehead-center and the uṣṇīṣa or crown-center [see pp. 114–116]. In the following stages of the meditation, one draws both the red and white bodhicitta through these centers. Eventually, as one progresses in the practice, one sucessively attains the ten Bodhisattva grounds. In the Kālacakra system, however, there exist two more Bodhisattva grounds.

In each of these energy-centers, there are 3600 drops of white element, the white bodhicitta. Corresponding to each of these 3600 drops are the 3600 immutable blisses. With each of these 3600 drops, there are 3600 material components of the body, as well as the 3600 active energies that are exhausted.

1) These drops of the white bodhicitta that lead to the immutable blisses first build up or draw together at the lowest, the genital-center and then, they gradually build up through the successive centers. This 'building up' [process] is like slowly pouring curd into a glass. As a result of retaining the 3600 drops of the white bodhicitta [without any emission whatsoever] in the genital-center, the corresponding 3600 immutable blisses arise and act as the antidotes that bring about the exhaustion of the 3600 material components of the body and the 3600 active energies. Through this achievement, one attains the first and the second Bodhisattva grounds called the Very Joyful and the Stainless [see above, p. 9].

2) Next, the 3600 drops of the white bodhicitta are drawn together or built up at the navel-center. As a result, there arise again the 3600 immutable blisses. And when this occurs at the navel, one attains the third and the fourth Bodhisattva grounds called the Luminous and the Radiant.

3) Then, one builds up the 3600 drops of the white bodhicitta at the heart-center. Like before , there occur the 3600 immutable blisses that act as the antidotes for the 3600 material components of the body and the 3600 active energies. It is by means of this that

one attains the fifth and the sixth Bodhisattva grounds called Difficult to Conquer and the Manifesting One.

4) The seventh and eighth Bodhisattva grounds [see above, pp. 9–10], called the Far Gone One and the Immovable, are attained when this process occurs at the throat-center.

5) A similar process has to take place at the forehead before one can attain the ninth and tenth Bodhisattva grounds called the Good Intelligence and the Cloud of Dharma.

6) The eleventh and the twelfth Bodhisattva grounds are attained after this process is completed at the crown-center.

In all, there are 21,600 drops of the white bodhicitta, 21,600 of the material components of the body and 21,600 of the active energies (i.e., 6 centers × 3600 = 21,600).

Simultaneous with this process of successively building up the white bodhicitta in the centers, starting from the bottom and ascending upward, is a complementary movement of the red bodhicitta that successively descends from the crown of the head, through these same energy-centers, to the genital-center. Again, this involves the 3600 sets [of the red drops] going down through the various energy-centers. Upon the conclusion of this ascending and descending process, again without allowing the red bodhicitta to be emitted, one experiences a supreme immutable bliss (Tib. mchog.tu.mi.'gyur.ba'i.bde.ba), with which all of the 21,600 material components of the body are exhausted. Because the white and red bodhicittas are also material aspects of the body, these too are extinguished at this time.

It would be a mistake to think that this process is like filling a pot or vessel with milk insofar as, at this point, the material components of the body are completely exhausted and one actualizes Kālacakra with consort, who are composed of just energy and consciousness, and one attains the 'rainbow body'. One can understand and see now that what needs to be done is to extinguish this material body which acts as a basis of suffering. If one exhausts or extinguishes this material body, then, of course, there is no basis for sickness.

It is true that the realizations of the stage of completion do not arise if one has not already gained the realizations of the stage of generation. The above explanation on the various stages of meditation is clearly on the stage of completion. Although we are not really fit to practice them yet, it would still be beneficial to contemplate the stages and to know the different Bodhisattva grounds. As one advances towards Buddhahood, the grounds will be the stages one will pass through. They can be thought of as signposts on a journey one is now in the process of making. In Tibet, for example, geshes and lamas had learned detailed descriptions of various holy places in India, such as the Vulture's Peak, Bodhagāya, Sarnath and so forth. Only words and imagination were involved. But then, later on, when they came down to India, they were actually able to visit these various places of pilgrimage, that they were already somewhat familiar with from the explanations they had previously received.

You are now, similarly, receiving a brief explanation of the stages of the Bodhisattva grounds, like names on a map. You can hear about them now and later on, when you actually attain them, you will remember, "Oh yes! Back there in Seattle, I remember him talking . . . " You are not always going to be in the situation in which you are now. If you continue your practice, eventually you will certainly become a Bodhisattva and head right on towards Buddhahood. It is a mistake to look upon the Buddhas or their images on the altar and to think of them as being 'way up in enlightenment,' whereas we are 'way down here' – as if there were no relationship between the two, or as if there were a great abyss separating us. This is simply not the case. We are related to the Buddhas. We are following the same path and when we come to the culmination of our own practice, we will be up there on the Dharma-throne giving our own teachings. So, through our own practice, it is definitely possible to attain Buddhahood.

For example, Je Tsongkhapa was once speaking to Mañjuśrī saying, "We used to be on a very equal plane. Both of us were wandering about in the cycle of existences. You, however, overcame self-cherishing and the false conception of the self and attained enlightenment. But here I am – still in the cycle of existences." Je Tsongkhapa practiced the above six branches of the Kālacakra yoga and had a vision of Kālacakra, who told him that he would be like Dawa Zangpo and would cause the Kālacakra teachings to flourish greatly.

Lama Drukpa Künleg, a great Kagyü master, also made a very similar statement when he addressed Jowo Śākyamuni, the Buddha in the central cathedral in Lhasa, "Previously, you had also been in the cycle of existences, but you practiced and gained realization; whereas I am still in samsāra. To you I prostrate." One could likewise look to the Buddha Śākyamuni. He was previously like ourselves, simply wandering about in the cycle of existences; but he met qualified spiritual mentors, especially the masters of the Mahāyāna and, having practiced, he attained enlightenment. As this has been true in the past, so is it still true for ourselves in the present. These individuals simply practiced with perseverance and enthusiasm and, therefore, attained enlightenment. We have been lagging behind and are left over. All of us are here to practice and those among us who do so with the greatest enthusiasm and perseverance will be the first to attain full enlightenment. And there will still be some of us left over. One should understand that enlightenment is attained through enthusiastic perseverance. Contemplating this, one should bolster up one's courage for the practice.

If one is engaing in a one-day tantric practice, it would be better to devote most of one's time to the practice of the stage of generation. Then, right at the end, give some time to the stage of completion. In this way, one has a rounded and complete tantric practice that places very important imprints upon the mind.

NOTES

[1]F. D. Lessing and A. Wayman, *Introduction to the Buddhist Tantric Systems* (Delhi: Motilal Banarsidass, 1980), p. 175: "The *prāṇa-āyāma* of the three lower Tantra divisions has different occasions, requirements, and methods of contemplation from the *prāṇa-āyāma* explained in the Anuttara [Tantra]."

[2]Gyalwa Gendun Drub, the First Dalai Lama, P. 144: "The *Guhyasamaja Tantra* states that the signs first arise at the eyebrows. The *Kalachakra Tantra* adds that because there are various types and levels of energies, there are also various places and times for the manifestation of the signs. For example, when the yogi cuts off the flow of the vital energies passing through the four petals of the four intermediate directions at the heart *chakra*, or the ru-pel, tsang - pa, *lha - chin*, and *nor-lay-gyal* energies, he experiences the signs of smoke, a mirage, radiant fireflies and a butter lamp. When he halts the flow of the equally abiding, upward flowing, all pervading and *lu* energies that flow through the four petals of the cardinal directions, he perceives the signs of Kalagni, the moon, the sun and Rahula [sic].

One then cuts off the flow of the life sustaining and downward moving energies which course above and below, thus experiencing the signs of lightning and the primordial drop."

[3]*Ibid.*, p. 146: "The physical position for performing the yoga of meditative stabilization is as previously explained.

Through application of this yoga one fills the skies with the various empty bodies and symbols previously generated within the mystic drop.

One then dissolves all these gods into one another and then into the Beatific Form of the *Sambhogakaya* as explained above, establishing the special divine pride until it effortlessly arises. When this divine pride dominates one's entire being, the yoga of meditative stabilization has been attained. One then is ready to enter into the third of the six yogas, that of energy concentration."

[4]*Ibid.*, p. 147: "One must here apply special techniques in order to bring the life sustaining and downward moving energies to the navel and to unify them accordingly.

The two main techniques used to bring about this union is [sic] the vajra recitation and the vase breathing. The method for applying these two yogic techniques for concentrating, holding and dissolving the vital energies are [sic] explained in the *Commentary to the Praise of Vajrapani.*"

[5]Keep clearly in mind that the Kālacakra system does not use this particular terminology of the 'five major' and 'five secondary' energies [see above, pp. 119–120].

[6]Ibid., p. 148: "In our tradition the vajra recitation is as explained in the *Commentary to the Praise of Chakrasambhara* and also Naropa's *Commentary to the Treatise on the Initiations.* When one meditates upon the yoga of energy concentration and casts the glance eliminating demons, one watches for the semblant and actual signs as explained previously in the yoga of sense withdrawal. One observes the empty body unified with the vital energies. The energies enter inside and are then made to arise with the luminosity of *om.* This is brought to the center of the pressure point at the crown, where rests the empty body that was previously produced through the first two yogas. This energy is then retained and made to arise with the luminosity of the letter *Hūṁ.* Together with the empty body it is then brought to the navel. As the energies are released, they are made to arise with the luminosity of the letter *Ah.* The strength of the flowing energies causes the empty body and so forth to move up the path of the central channel to the upper aperture, where they exit.

Through repeated meditation, the inhalation and exhalation periods gradually decrease and the period of retention increases until one is eventually able to retain the application of the empty body and the vital energies at the navel for long periods of time.

After the vajra recitation technique has been mastered one can take up the practice of vase breathing."

[7]Garma C. C. Chang, *Teachings on Tibetan Yoga* (The Citadel Press, Secaucus, New Jersey, 1977), p. 56.

SECTION TEN

We should engage in whichever of our practices we are presently capable of following with full diligence. Those that we are not able to practice at this time should not be simply disregarded but, rather, we should offer prayers that we may be able to follow them either in the latter part of this life or in future lives. While keeping hold of this aspiration, let us engage in practices designed to further purify the mind and accumulate merit.

The Bodhisattva Śāntideva quotes the Buddha, who is totally free from any fraudulence and teaches very honestly and straightforwardly, – stating that even insects are endowed with Buddha-Nature and, therefore, have the ability to attain full enlightenment. If this is true for insects, then it goes without saying that human beings, who are likewise endowed with Buddha-Nature and, in addition, have the ability to recognize and avoid that which is harmful and engage in that which is beneficial, certainly have the ability to attain enlightenment. This is within reach if we simply maintain enthusiasm and perseverence in the practice.

Śāntideva further states that if people holding very ordinary vocations, such as fishermen, carpenters or loggers, give so much effort and endure great hardships of heat and cold for relatively minor aims of this life alone, then those of us who are striving towards full enlightenment should certainly be able to take on the hardships involved in the practice. So, Śāntideva asks a rhetorical question, "Why is it that you, who are seeking full enlightenment for the benefit of all creatures, are not able to bear these hardships?"

149

2. THE DAYTIME YOGA

A brief explanation of the night yoga has already been given. Now, we continue with the explanation of the daytime yoga.

a. THE PLACE OF THE PRACTICE

First of all, one should meditate in a place surrounded by walls, but with no roof so that it is open at the top. One should be facing in such a way that the sun is behind one, snow mountains or bodies of water are not in one's vision, and the wind is not blowing against one's face.

b. THE POSTURE

The physical posture [that one assumes] during the meditation is that of the vajra posture, with the hands either in meditative equipoise or clenched into a fist, thumbs tucked in. All aspects of the posture are the same as described previously for the night yoga [see above, p. 134, b].

c. THE ACTUAL PRACTICE

The meditation is also the same as described for the night yoga. One visualizes the body of empty form of the deity and consort in the central channel, between the eyebrows.

There are also the six branches of the meditation. The above visualization is done in the first stage, the stage of individual convergence. During the second stage, the individual stability, one stabilizes what has been accomplished during the first branch of the practice. All of the ensuing five branches of the practice after the first one has been attained, are simply to further develop and increase this first practice.

d. THE FUNCTION OF THE SIX BRANCHES

Although the following material has already been taught and we have become familiar with it, it is helpful to hear it again [and again], and to have the mental imprints [on our continuum].

150

1) & 2) Since individual convergence is the practice which initially actualizes the body of empty form in the central channel at the forehead opening, and individual stability creates firmness/stability, these first two branches of the practice make the various active energies serviceable.

3) The third stage of the practice, the life-effort, blocks the two side channels, the roma and the kyangma, causing the energies to abide in the central channel. Thus, the chief practices of the life-effort branch of the yoga are designed to draw together the downward-clearing energy and the life-sustaining energy. These practices are the vajra recitation of the Oṃ, Āḥ, Hūṃ mantra and the vase-like meditation, both of which have been described previously.

4) The next stage of the practice, retention, occurs after one has already drawn the energies into the central channel and is somewhat able to make them abide there. The function of the retention branch is to stabilize the retention of the energies in the very center of the central channel – to make them firmly abide there.

5) In the recollection branch of the practice, one goes into union with one of the three types of consorts, literally called 'mudrās': the Action Mudrā (Skt. karma-mudrā; Tib. las-.kyi.phyag.rgya), who is an actual person, a consort brought to one by one's karma; the Wisdom Mudrā (Skt. jñāna-mudrā; Tib. ye.shes.kyi.phyag.rgya), who is a visualized appearance in the meditator's mind – the union with her takes place during the visualization; the Great Mudrā (Skt. mahā-mudrā; Tib. phyag.r-gya.chen.po), the consort of Kālacakra, Natsog Yum, whose body is the body of empty form. A practitioner of dull faculties enters into union with the Action Mudrā; a person with medium faculties goes into union with the Wisdom Mudrā; and a practitioner of the sharpest faculties with Great Mudrā Natsog Yum.

While one is in union with any of these three types of consorts on this stage of the practice, the white bodhicitta melts from the crown-center, descends to the tip of the genitals, where it is retained and, in this way, one experiences the immutable bliss.

However, in order to engage in a practice such as entering into union with the Action Mudrā, rather than the Wisdom Mudrā, several qualifications are indispensable:

151

a) one ought to have trained one's mind on the common path;
b) one ought to have perfectly received the empowerment;
c) one must be maintaining the precepts and pledges;
d) the male and the female practitioners ought to be at the same level of realization; one's realization should not be higher than that of the other. For example, if the yogin, the male practitioner, has attained a level in the stage of completion called 'mind-liberation,' then his consort, the yoginī, should also have attained that same degree of realization. When both are of equal realization, by engaging in this practice, the male practitioner increases the female's realization, and the female increases the male's realization. Enlightenment for both of them is soon attained.

It is very important to understand the purpose of this type of meditation, that is, the male and female practicing in union. This is a very profound practice coming from Vajradhara. Milarepa, speaking on this critical point, said that in the practice, one meditates using the channels, the energies and the drops, and that one should, at the proper time, practice with an Action Mudrā; however, one must do so in a fully qualified way. If one does not, practicing prematurely leads to birth in a hell. It is also said that, as a result of such a malpractice, one remains in the hell for as long as space lasts.

There is much to be explained about the recollection branch of the practice. In fact, one could spend many, many days just explaining this because it is very extensive. One aspect of this practice is that of gazing upon Natsog Yum, the consort of Kālacakra, [through which one experiences] the spontaneous bliss (Tib. lhan.skyes.kyi.bde.ba) and the rising of the tum.mo flame. This melts the white bodhicitta at the crown, which then descends through the various energy-centers where one experiences the four types of joy: the joy (Skt. ānanda; Tib. dga'.ba), the supreme joy (Skt. parama-ānanda; Tib. mchog.dga'); the extraordinary joy (Skt. virama-ānanda; Tib. khyad.dga') and the spontaneous joy (Skt. sahaja-ānanda; Tib. lhan.skyes.kyi.dga'.ba) [see above, p. 11, 3].

The preceding are the first five branches of the practice by means of which one accomplishes concentration, the sixth branch of the yoga of Kālacakra.

6) The single-pointed union of the emptiness of all phenomena and the mind that is realizing that emptiness constitutes the sixth branch [of the Kālacakra yoga]. The second way of understanding this branch of the practice is as follows: it is the union of the emptiness of all phenomena appearing in the divine form of the consort Natsog Yum, who is the nature of wisdom, and the supreme immutable bliss (Tib. mchog.tu.mi.'gyur.ba'i.bde.ba) that appears in the divine form of Kālacakra. Thus the union of the wisdom realizing emptiness symbolized by the consort, and the mind of the supreme immutable bliss embodied in the deity Kālacakra is also called the concentration branch of this yoga of the Kālacakra (cf. above, p. 133, 6].

One should keep in mind that the union of the deity and consort is not like mundane sexual intercourse; it symbolizes the union of method and wisdom, where the deity Kālacakra embodies the method and the consort Natsog Yum embodies the wisdom aspect of the teachings [cf. p. 60, 7]. As a result of one's going into union with one of the three types of consorts, the Action Mudrā, the Wisdom Mudrā or the Great Mudrā, the immutable bliss (Tib. mi.'gyur.ba'i.bde.ba) arises and is then increased more and more.

This brief explanation of the six branches of the yoga of Kālacakra completes the exposition of the various stages of meditation. The next topic to be explained is the attainment of full enlightenment in this practice of Kālacakra.

IV. THE STAGE OF MANIFESTING THE RESULT

A. A GENERAL PRESENTATION OF THE HIGHEST YOGA TANTRA

There is a general presentation of the Highest Yoga Tantra (Skt. anuttara-yoga-tantra; Tib. rnal.'byor.bla.med) such as is found, for example, in the Hevajra and the Vajrayoginī practices. Let us look at the Hevajra practice where there are three primary steps in the tantric practice, particularly on the stage of completion: the

153

attainment of the illusory body, the attainment of the clear light, the union.

1. If one has attained the illusory body, it is then completely certain that one will attain enlightenment in that particular life. The attainment of the illusory body with regard to Hevajra does not mean that this body becomes Hevajra but, rather, that one attains or actualizes, apart from this gross body of flesh and bones, the Hevajra Body marked with various major and minor signs and which is to be understood in terms of 12 analogies.

The illusory body that one emanates as can go to different places, such as the Pure Lands, and make offerings to the beings there. However, to be of direct service to the gross beings here, one has to have a gross body and [with that motivation in mind] one brings back and dissolves the illusory body into one's gross body [see p. 109]. Then, one can teach Dharma or do whatever one wants to do.

QUESTION: "What about in the Kālacakra system? After you have completely exhausted this [gross] body, how can you directly help people?"

ANSWER: "That is a very easy question because, after you attain enlightenment, you can manifest, emanate yourself, as many times as you like and serve in that way. You are a Buddha and, in just a moment, you can emanate yourself all over the place."

2. Following the illusory body is the attainment of the clear light which is twofold: the subjective clear light. The objective clear light is the mind which realizes emptiness.

3. The union refers to the union of the illusory body and the clear light. That is the essence of the stage of completion.

If one asks, "Is meditation on emptiness a practice on the stage of completion?" one must reply, "No, it is not, because meditation on emptiness also occurs in the sūtra practice." Then one might further ask, "Is meditation focusing on the energies a practice of the stage of completion?" one must again answer, "No, it is not." Why? Because such meditation on the energies is also found in the practices of the lower three classifications of tantra. There are many meditations on these energies also found in the non-Buddhist practices. Deity meditation also is not an exclusive practice of the stage of completion either, because those who are still practicing on the stage of generation are certainly engaging in deity meditation.

So, what are the stages of generation and completion? A definition of the stage of generation has already been given. Can anyone remember it?

STUDENT: "I think it is the purification of birth, death and bardo."

GESHE DHARGYEY: "That would equally apply, or even more so, to the stage of completion because it is the stage of completion which actually brings about the purification of death, bardo and birth."

One should at least know the definitions and understand the differences between the two stages of the path. Here is a rough translation of the stage of generation:

An artificial or constructed meditation involving visualization which follows the parallels of the processes of death, bardo and birth without drawing energies into the central channel [cf. p. 83].

And here is a rough definition of the stage of completion: The entering, abiding and dissolving of the energies in the central channel by means of non-artificial meditation. More specifically, it is the focusing upon the vital points of the vajra-body in order to draw the energies into the central channel.

B. ATTAINMENT OF FULL ENLIGHTENMENT THROUGH THE KĀLACAKRA PRACTICE

In the general outline of the teachings that has been followed over the past weeks, there was first the presentation of the basis [I. A. and B.]. Following this, there were the teachings on vows and pledges [II. A. and B.], then the presentation of the path of meditation consisting of the stage of generation [III. A.] and the stage of completion [III. B.]. We will discuss now the stage of manifesting the result, which is the attainment of full enlightenment in the practice of the Kālacakra.

Having, first of all, trained one's mind in the common path by means of the cultivation of renunciation, bodhicitta and the realistic view, one then needs to properly receive an empowerment. Then, one trains in the stage of generation: first in the gross and then the subtle stages. Having come to the culmination of the subtle stage, one engages in the practice of the stage of completion consisting of the six branches of the yoga that have just been described. In doing so, one focuses on the six essential points of the energy-centers: the genital, navel and so forth. In this process, one gradually builds up the white bodhicitta and, at the same time, causes the descent of the red bodhicitta in these successive centers. Throughout this process, the bodhicitta is not allowed to be emitted and, as a result, the active energies and the material constituents of the body are gradually extinguished. Finally, the red and white bodhicitta themselves are extinguished. Upon the conclusion of this practice, one attains the body of empty form, which is like the colors of a rainbow.

The Buddha Vajradhara was extremely kind to sentient beings to reveal this very profound practice of tantra. It is truly like a gold-transforming elixir that is able to turn copper and other base metals into gold. With this practice of tantra, one is able to transform one's body, which is presently of a gross material nature and therefore subject to suffering and sickness, by exhausting its material components, and also to transform the 'primordial mind' (Tib. gnyug.ma'i.sems) and the 'primordial body' into the nature of the deity and consort. In this material body, there are active energies that cause the arisal of such mental distortions as anger, attachment and so forth. In the process [of transmutation], these active energies are extinguished.

It is important to understand what is being translated here as the 'primordial mind' and 'primordial body':

The primordial mind (or stream of consciousness) is the very subtle mind which has always been with us.

The primordial body is the very subtle life-sustaining energy that accompanies the primordial mind and has, likewise, always been with us.

It is these that are transformed into the nature of the deity whose body is composed of only consciousness and energy.

To understand this, imagine that there are people who have always lived here in Seattle. You could say that they are like the primordial inhabitants, the native inhabitants of Seattle. People who just come in, like transients, could be considered the adventitious inhabitants of Seattle. So, likewise, each of us is endowed with both consciousness and the life-sustaining energy that are primordial in the sense that we have always had them. Most of the components of our being, like our sensory perceptions, most of the factors of mental consciousness, the gross body and so forth, are simply temporary aggregates that we have for a short time. But, as has been explained previously, these are shed in the death process and the various sense perceptions become latent. After the period of gloom or darkness in the death process, the very subtle primordial mind and the primordial body (or life-sustaining energy) manifest. It is these that carry on from lifetime to lifetime, whereas the other aggregates do not.

With the culmination of this tantric path, one actualizes the body of empty form of the deity and consort and attains the consciousness that simultaneously directly experiences all phenomena and is, itself, of the nature of the great immutable bliss. Upon this attainment, one has become a fully enlightened Buddha and one has attained the 'seven-branch union' or, more literally, the 'seven-branch kiss', which refers to the union of the deity and consort. Futhermore, one attains the four-fold Body of the Buddha: the Emanation Body, the Enjoyment Body the Wisdom Truth Body and the Nature Truth Body (see above p. 12). Being a Buddha, one is now immensely capable of serving sentient beings. In just one instant, one is able to emanate oneself in many, many ways throughout the world in order to be of service to sentient beings.

In the present situation, while still unenlightened, one does not have a very great capacity for serving the needs of sentient beings; one is simply not terribly effective. Upon the attainment of enlightenment, one has brought this ability to fulfillment and one will spontaneously and continuously have this perfected ability until all sentient beings are enlightened.

As explained previously, there are two types of methods for attaining Buddhahood in the tantric practice. In the Guhyasamāja practice, for example, one actualizes the illusory body apart from the gross body and, in this way, attains full enlightenment. In contrast, in the Kālacakra system one actually extinguishes this

157

material body and actualizes the body of the deity and consort. Both of these methods are perfectly authentic and they are completely effective.

The mere fact that there are different ways of teaching, or different ways of guiding a yogin or a yoginī through these tantric practices does not mean that they are actually contradictory or that they are leading to different attainments. They are different, but they are not contradictory. They lead to exactly the same state of full enlightenment. This would be like having one room with different doors. Are the doors the same? No. Nevertheless, if you pass through any of the doors, you come into the room and the room is the same. Although there are different methods within the practice of tantra leading to full enlightenment, the state of full enlightenment is the same.

A parallel can be found in the four spiritual traditions of Tibet. Each of them has its own name for different reasons: Nyingma is named after their following of the old translations of the tantras; Sakya is named after the region, specifically, the terrain of that region; Kagyü is named after their holding of the four oral lineages; Gelug is named after the name of a monastery. So, it is simply a question of different names. There are slight variations in the customs, in the emphasis, or in the traditions of the lamas of these different traditions; but, in essence, they all go back to the teachings of the Buddha and each offers an authentic means for the attainment of full enlightenment. One needs to understand that the mere fact that they are different does not mean that they are contradictory, that one has to be right and the others have to be wrong.

Nāgārjuna has stated that if one does not have sharp faculties and is not very intelligent, it is difficult to progress on the path. Why? Because one finds in the Dharma teachings that sometimes the Buddha states that phenomena are inherently existent and sometimes he states that they are not inherently existent. Consequently, if one is a person of dull faculties, one might simply be left with confusion, thinking that sometimes Buddha said this and sometimes he said that, both of which seem to be contradictory. One might get all mixed up While on the contrary, a person with sharp faculties will be able to pierce through [these seemingly contradictory statements] and come up with the actual meaning. Thus, if one looks at these various traditions or the various means of guiding disciples with sharp faculties with clear intelligence, then one's understanding becomes greater and greater.

One should understand the teachings of the Buddha to be like a medicine given to specific patients. Just as the medicine will vary from one patient to another, so do the teachings vary from one disciple to another. Take, for example, a person who is suffering from a very drastic heat disorder. While the heat is very dominant, a qualified physician will tell that person to avoid taking any meat or alcohol. However, let us imagine that his heat disorder has died down, but a wind or energy disorder has arisen. That same doctor might now tell that same patient, "You should now have meat and alcohol." There is no actual contradiction here because these substances once harmful, can be beneficial at another time.

In like manner, the Buddha states very frequently in the *Vinaya Sūtras* [scriptures on the monastic discipline] that the monks should take absolutely no alcohol and should not have any sexual intercourse or relationships with women. In fact, they should not even be alone in the same room with a woman. This is very emphatically and repeatedly stated – it is very strict. This is meant for beings who are still subject to taking lower rebirth as a result of such actions. However, monks who have gone quite far in their practice and have gained very high states of realization in terms of bodhicitta, realization of emptiness, as well as their practices of tantra, are allowed by the Buddha to have sexual intercourse with women and to take alcohol. The reason is that at a certain stage of practice, when one is sufficiently advanced, these same activities can further one towards the attainment of full enlightenment. Consequently, there is not actually any contradiction here at all. If one really looks into this with intelligence, one feels greater and greater faith rather than confusion.

Take the analogy of the peacock that is able to eat poison. As poison nourishes him, his feathers become all the more bright, shiny and colorful. Whereas, if a crow should look at what the peacock is doing and take the same poison, he would keel over dead. In like manner, if beginning practitioners like ourselves should try to take on some of the practices of the very highly advanced beings, this would be to our detriment rather than benefit. The five ambrosias are literally substances such as excrement, urine and so forth. A highly realized yogin is able to transform them and actually experience great bliss. If one has attained that stage, where one can transform such substances, then one has a free allowance in terms of what may be done.

This completes the teaching on the Kālacakra. The last few lectures have been on the stage of completion. We cannot meditate now on this stage properly and expect to gain the realizations. The best we can do is offer prayers that we may eventually be qualified to follow such practices. And for now, we can do just a little bit of this practice simply to place beneficial imprints upon our mind-streams but it cannot be the main practice yet. What should be emphasized above all in our present practice is keeping the tantric pledges and precepts, for it is stated that if one manages not to incur any of the tantric downfalls over a period of 16 lifetimes, even if one is not engaging in the practice of meditation, simply keeping the precepts purely, within 16 lives, one will attain full enlightenment.

I received the Kālacakra empowerment first from Lhatsün Dorje Chang. He was a very great lama in Tibet, a Root-guru of the Junior Tutor of His Holiness the Dalai Lama, and was considered a sage by the lamas of all spiritual traditions in Tibet. His Holiness has frequently said, "It is a very great pity that it was not possible for Lhatsün Dorje Chang to come to India."

I also received the Kālacakra empowerment three or four times from His Holiness the Dalai Lama. His Holiness received the empowerment and the teaching from his Senior Tutor, Kyabje Yongdzin Ling Dorje Chang. Kyabje Yongdzin Ling Dorje Chang received the empowerment and teaching of Kalacakra from Kyabje Kangsar Dorje Chang [see p. 15]. It was said that he was a manifestation of Mañjuśrī. The lineage goes back in an unbroken succession from lama to lama to the Buddha Vajradhara [Dorje Chang]. Within the context of tantra, it is necessary for there to occur this unbroken continuum of the lineage which always goes back to Vajradhara.

We strongly believe that the Buddhist teachings are still present due to the kindness of His Holiness the Dalai Lama. We should all offer prayers for his long life.

We should further offer prayers for the long life of both Venerable Dagchen Rinpoche and Dagmo Kusho, as well as for the flourishing of their activities. It was due to their kindness that we have had the place for these teachings to be imparted.

Furthermore, in making this series of teachings possible, many people have given their time and made great efforts in making the necessary arrangements, and we should offer prayers also that their practice might continue, prosper and be free of obstacles. In short, we should offer prayers that their minds turn to Dharma, and that their Dharma may progress on the path, and be free of obstacles. Please offer such prayers. This course has gone very well – free from interruption, free of major illness, free of other kinds of obstructions. The fact that it has gone so well is due to the efforts of the people involved.

I have been teaching Westerners for quite a few years now. And over the years, I have been repeatedly asked to come to the West, but my answer was always, "No. What would be the benefit? I cannot speak their language." But then, when this situation was presented and His Holiness asked me, not once but twice, saying that it would be most beneficial if I were to come to the West and especially to give these Kālacakra teachings, thinking of the great benefit of following the instructions of one's guru, I decided that this would be good to do. Due to the kindness of all these individuals, I myself have been able to accrue great merit.

As I said before, all of you have a very good situation here in which to practice Dharma. Obviously, during the daytime, you have your jobs that you need to do. But, when your daily work is finished, you can come to this center to receive teachings, meditate and practice according to your abilities. This is extremely good. When a person does not receive teachings for quite some time, the mind tends to grow rough, more barbaric. With teaching, the mind is once again cultivated for the Dharma. It is like the grass in a meadow: if rain does not fall for a long time, it tends to wither. So it is the same for the mind – that is its nature. Do not let your aspiration to practice dwindle, but rather encourage it, foster it so that it grows stronger and stronger!

One further point is the importance of having the company of other people who are following spiritual practice. This can be very helpful. In contrast, if one becomes very intimate with those who have no regard for spiritual practice, this tends to harm one's own practice. Therefore, where possible, associate with people who are following the path.

There is an account of two men in Pempo, an area to the north of Lhasa in Tibet. One was a heavy drinker and the other was not. They split up. The drunkard went to Reting Monastery and there encountered a very fine lama who told him of the disadvantages of alcoholism and taught him how to follow spiritual practice. He gave up drinking and became a very fine practitioner. The non-drinker went down to Lhasa, and there he got in to the company of a bunch of drunkards. He started "hitting the sauce," and made of big habit of it and became, more or less, an alcoholic. This indicates the strong influence of people with whom one associates.

To give one more analogy, if you are in a place that is all black (with soot on the walls) and you move around, you end up all black. Whereas, if you are in a place that is all white (with whitewash on the walls, as in India), then you end up all white. Likewise, if one associates with smokers, one becomes a smoker; if one associates with snuffers, one becomes a snuff-inhaler. Generally, bad qualities tend to be contagious. If you can associate with people who are following good practice, it is very helpful.

Where there is the Mahāyāna Dharma, the main practice is the cultivation of bodhicitta which should be the central pillar of our practice. This center, Sakya Tegchen Choling, "The Place of the Mahāyāna Dharma," is very well named. Venerable Dagchen Rinpoche and Dagmo Kusho have been extremely skillful in their strong emphasis on Avalokiteśvara practice. It is stated that Avalokiteśvara is the divine embodiment and the essence of all the Buddhas; the six syllable mantra, Oṃ Maṇi Padme Hūṃ, is the essence of all mantras; and the very essence of all Dharma is bodhicitta. Having this as the very center of one's practice is an extremely, skillful approach. The master Rāhulagupta told Atīśa, who had a very profound samādhi, "Even if you have such a degree of samādhi that a person could beat a drum right next to your ear and you wouldn't even hear it, nevertheless, this will not be sufficient for attaining the paths or Bodhisattva grounds. Rather, devote yourself to the cultivation of bodhicitta. Devote yourself to Avalokiteśvara, who is the divine embodiment of the compassion of all the Buddhas."

As one great Tibetan lama stated, "Even if one has a whole valley filled with gold, one would not be able to take even the tiniest bit with one at the point of death. Whereas, simply reciting the mantra Oṃ Maṇi Padme Hūṃ once is something that is of benefit in this life and beyond, after death." One should not have the idea that the Oṃ Maṇi Padme Hūṃ recitation is a very simple practice for simple-minded people or amateurs in the Dharma. Rather, the mantra is very profound. In one context, it embodies the method and wisdom aspects of the teaching. In terms of the lower two classifications of tantra, it embodies the practices of 'with sign' and 'without sign.' In terms of the Highest Yoga Tantra, it embodies both the stages of generation and completion. A qualified master could spend six or seven years giving the full implications of just this one very profound mantra.

Nowadays, there is a lot of talk about the need for world peace. Nevertheless, it is not happening. Why is it not happening? Because no matter how much people talk about it, as long as minds are still dominated by such mental distortions as attachment and anger, peace is an impossibility. You can drink all the tea you like, and still the anger is not abated. You can eat as much as you want, but still the anger is not abated. Anger and the other mental distortions decrease through the practice of the Buddha's teachings. Here, we have the possibility to do something effica-cious for world peace by subduing these mental distortions in our own minds. Further, while engaging in the practice oneself, if one encourages other people who are not in the Dharma to enter into the practice, this is also very helpful and important to do.

In conclusion, one of the responsibilites for those of us who are practicing Dharma is to avert war especially world war by continually offering very strong prayers that such an event may be avoided. Let us do so!

BIBLIOGRAPHY AND RECOMMENDED FURTHER READING

1. A-kya Young-dzin Yang-chän Ga-wäi Lo-dro'ö.
   A Compendium of Ways of Knowing: A Clear Mirror of What Should Be Accepted and Rejected. With Commentary Compiled from Oral Teachings by Geshe Ngawang Dhargyey (trans. and ed. Sherpa Tulku and Alexander Berzin with Khamlung Tulku and Jonathan Landaw). Dharamsala: Library of Tibetan Works and Archives, 1976.

2. Amipa, Sherab Gyaltsen.
   A Waterdrop from the Glorious Sea: A Concise Account of the Advent of Buddhism in General and the Teachings of the Sakyapa Tradition in Particular (trans. Gelong Jhampa Kelsang). Rikon: Tibet Institute, 1976.

3. Aśvaghoṣa.
   The Buddhacarita: Or, Acts of the Buddha (trans. E. H. Johnston). Lahore, 1936; rpt. Delhi: Motilal Banarsidass, 1978.

4. Batchelor, Stephen (trans.).
   A Guide to the Bodhisattva's Way of Life by Achārya Shāntideva. 1979; rpt. Dharamsala: LTWA, 1981.

5. ———.
   Alone with Others: An Existential Approach to Buddhism. New York: Grove Press, Inc., 1983.

6. Bendall, Cecil and W. H. D. Rouse (trans.).
   Śikshāsamuccaya: A Compendium of Buddhist Doctrine Compiled by Śāntideva Chiefly from Earlier Mahāyāna Sūtras. London: Indian Text Series, 1922; [rpt.] Delhi: Motilal Banarsidass, 1971.

7. Beresford, Brian C. (trans. and ed.).
   Mahāyāna Purification: "The Confession Sūtra" with Commentary by Ārya Nagārjuna and "The Practice of Vajrasattva" with Sādhana, Supplemented by Verbally Transmitted Commentaries from Geshe Ngawang Dhar-

gyey, Geshe Rabten, Gegan Khyentse and Thubten Zopa Rinpoche. Dharamsala: LTWA, 1980.

8. Berzin, Alexander (trans. and ed.).
The Four-Themed Precious Garland: An Introduction to Dzog-ch'en, the Great Completeness by Long-chen Rabjam-pa Dr'i-me wö-zer, with Explanation and Oral Commentary by His Holiness Dudjom Rinpoche and Beru Khyentze Rinpoche. Dharamsala: LTWA, 1979.

9. ——.
"The Mahāmudrā Eliminating the Darkness of Ignorance": by the Ninth Kar-ma-pa Wang-ch'ug Dor-je with Commentary Given Orally by Beru Khyentze Rinpoche and *"Fifty Stanzas of Guru Devotion"* by Aśvaghoṣa with Commentary Given Orally by Geshe Ngawang Dhargyey. Dharamsala: LTWA, 1978.

10. Buddhaghosa, Bhadantācariya.
The Path of Purification: Visuddhimagga (trans. Bhikkhu Ñyāṇamoli). 2 vols. Sri Lanka, 1956; rpt. Berkeley and London: Shambhala, 1976.

11. Chang, Garma C.C. (trans.).
Teachings of Tibetan Yoga. Secaucus: The Citadel Press, 1977.

12. ——.
The Hundred Thousand Songs of Milarepa. New Hyde Park, 1962; rpt. Boulder: Shambhala, 1977.

13. Chögyal Phagpa, VIIth Patriarch of Sakya.
A Gift of Dharma to Kublai Khan (trans. Āchārya Lobsang Jamspal and Achārya Mañjusiddhārtha). Victoria, B.C.: Buddhist Dharma Society, 1976.

14. Conze, Edward.
Buddhist Thought in India. London, 1962; rpt. Ann Arbor Paperbacks, 1973.

15. ——.
Buddhist Meditation. London, 1956; rpt. New York: Harper & Row, 1975.

16. ——.
A Short History of Buddhism. 1980; rpt. London: Unwin Paperbacks, 1982.

165

17. —— (trans.).
Abhisamayālaṅkāra. Roma: Istituto Italiano per il Medio ed Estremo Oriente, 1954.
18. —— (trans.).
The Perfection of Wisdom in Eight Thousand Lines. 1973; rpt. San Francisco: Four Seasons Foundation, 1983.
19. —— (trans.).
Buddhist Wisdom Books: Vajracchedika and Prajñā-āramitāhrdaya. London: Allen & Unwin, 1958.
20. —— (trans.).
Buddhist Scriptures. 1959; rpt. Harmondsworth: Penguin Books Ltd., 1975.
21. —— (ed.).
Buddhist Texts Through the Ages. Oxford, 1954; rpt. New York: Harper & Row, 1964.
22. Dalai Lama, The 1st – Drub, Gyalwa Gendun.
"To Entice the Minds of the Wise": Notes on the Two Stages of Yogic Application in the Kalachakra Tantra. In *Bridging the Sutras and Tantras: A collection of Ten Minor Works* (comp. and ed. Glenn H. Mullin et alii). India, 1981; Ithaca, N.Y.: Gabriel Press, 1982.
23. Dalai Lama, The IIIrd – Gyatso, Sonam.
Essence of Refined Gold: Commentary by Tenzin Gyatso, the Fourteenth Dalai Lama Including "Song of the Stages in Spiritual Practice" by Tsong Khapa and "A Lam Rim Preliminary Rite" by Gyalwa Sonam Gyatso (trans. and ed. Glenn H. Mullin). Ithaca, N.Y.: Gabriel Press, 1982.
24. Dalai Lama, The Vth – [Gyatso, Ngawang Lopsang].
Practice of Emptiness: The Perfection of Wisdom Chapter of the Fifth Dalai Lama's "Sacred Word of Mañjuśrī" (trans. Jeffrey Hopkins in accordance with instruction from Geshe Rapden).1974; revised ed. Dharamsala: LTWA, 1976.
25. Dalai Lama, The XIVth – Gyatso, Tenzin.
The Opening of the Wisdom Eye. Wheaton, Ill.: Theosophical Publishing House, 1972.

26. ——.
Concerning the Kalachakra Initiation in America (trans.
L.T. Doboom Tulku and Glenn Mullin). Madison: Deer
Park, 1981.

27. ——.
"The Guru Yoga of Kalachakra in Connection With the
Six Sessions in Completely Facilitating Form": Versified
by Kyab-je Ling Rinpoche (trans. Jeffrey Hopkins). In
Kalachakra Initiation: Madison, 1981. Madison: Deer
Park, 1981.

28. ——.
The Buddhism of Tibet and the Key to the Middle Way
(translated in the main by Jeffrey Hopkins and Lati
Rinpoche). The Wisdom of Tibet Series, I. London:
George Allen and Unwin Ltd., 1975.

29. ——.
My Land and My People. New York: Potala Corporation,
1977.

30. ——.
Universal Responsibility and the Good Heart. Dharamsala:
LTWA, 1980.

31. ——.
The Key to Madhyamika (trans. Gonsar Tulku with the
Assistance of Gavin Kilty). 1974; revised ed. Dharamsala:
LTWA, 1976.

32. ——.
An Introduction to Buddhism. Delhi: Tibet House, [1965].

33. ——.
"A Meditation on Compassion": From a Discourse by His
Holiness the 14th Dalai Lama together with a Sādhana of
Avalokiteśhvara. In Āryaśūra's "Aspiration": with Com-
mentary by Gen-dun Gyatso, the 2nd Dalai Lama and "A
Meditation on Compassion" (trans. and ed. Brian C.
Beresford with L.T. Doboom Tulku, Gonsar Tulku,
Sherpa Tulku). 1979; 2nd ed. Dharamsala: LTWA, 1978.

34. Dayal, Har.
The Bodhisattva Doctrine in Buddhist Sanskrit Literature.
1932, rpt. Delhi: Motilal Banarsidass, 1975.

35. De Bary, William T. (ed.).
    The Buddhist Tradition. New York: Vintage Books, 1972.
36. ——and A.T. Embree (eds.).
    A Guide to Oriental Classics. 2nd ed. New York and London: Columbia University Press, 1975.
37. Dhargyey, Geshe Ngawang.
    Tibetan Tradition of Mental Development: Oral Teachings of Tibetan Lama [trans. Sherpa Tulku and Khamlung Tulku. Dharamsala: LTWA, 1974.
38. ——.
    "An Introduction to the Kalachakra Initiation" (trans. Translation Bureau of the LTWA). In *Kalachakra Initiation: Madison 1981*. Madison: Deer Park, 1981.
39. ——.
    Taking the Bodhicitta Vows. (Prepared by the Translation Bureau of the Library of Tibetan Works and Archives of His Holiness the Dalai Lama). Dharamsala: LTWA, 1974.
40. Dharmaraksita.
    The Wheel of Sharp Weapons: A Mahayana Training of the Mind. (Translation of the Tibetan "Theg-pa-chen-pohi-blo-sbyong Mtson-cha-hkhor-lo" by Dharmaraksita prepared by Geshe Ngawang Dhargye, Sherpa Tulku, Khamlung Tulku, Alexander Berzin and Jonathan Landaw). Dharamsala: LTWA, 1976. Revised, with commentary 1981.
41. Dönden, Dr. Yeshi.
    The Ambrosia Heart Tantra (trans. Ven. Jhampa Kelsang). Dharamsala: LTWA, 1977.
42. Dowman, Keith (trans.).
    The Legend of the Great Stupa: The Life Story of the Lotus Born Guru. Emeryville: Dharma Publishing, 1973.
43. Dumoulin, Heinrich and John C. Maraldo (eds.).
    Buddhism in the Modern World. Breisgau, 1970; English trans. New York: MacMillan Publishing Co., Inc., 1976.
44. Evans-Wentz, W.Y. (ed.).
    Tibetan Yoga and the Secret Doctrines: Or Seven Books of Wisdom of the Great Path, According to the Lama Kazi Dawa-Samdup's English Rendering. 1935; rpt. London: Oxford University Press, 1958.

45. —— (ed.).
The Tibetan Book of the Great Liberation. London: Oxford University Press, 1935.

46. Fremantle, Francesca and Chögyam Trungpa (trans.).
The Tibetan Book of the Dead: The Great Liberation through-Hearing in the Bardo, by Guru Rinpoche According to Karma Lingpa. Berkeley: Shambhala, 1975.

47. sGam.po.pa.
The Jewel Ornament of Liberation (trans. Herbert V. Guenther). 1959; [rpt.] Berkeley: Shambhala, 1971.

48. Gard, Richard A. (ed.).
Buddhism: The Way of Buddhism: Its Ideals and Philosophy, Its Religious and Moral Principles and Practices, Its Implications in the Political, Social and Cultural Life of Its Followers. New York: George Braziller, 1962.

49. Goldstein, Joseph.
The Experience of Insight: A Simple and Direct Guide to Buddhist Meditation. Boulder and London: Shambhala, 1983.

50. Govinda, Lama Anagarika.
The Psychological Attitude of Early Buddhist Philosophy: and Its Systematic Representation According to Abhidhamma Tradition. London, 1961; New York: Samuel Weiser, 1974.

51. ——.
Foundations of Tibetan Mysticism: According to the Esoteric Teachings of the Great Mantra Oṁ Maṇi Padme Hūm. York Beach, Maine: Samuel Weiser, Inc., 1982.

52. Guenther, Herbert V. (trans.).
The Life and Teachings of Nāropa. London, 1963; rpt. New York: Oxford University Press, 1975.

53. ——.
and Leslie S. Kawamura (trans.). *Mind in Buddhist Psychology: A Translation of Ye-shes Rgyalmtshan's "The Necklace of Clear Understanding."* Emeryville: Dharma Publishing, 1975.

54. ——.
Philosophy and Psychology in the Abhidharma. India, 1974; rpt. Berkeley: Shambhala, 1976.

169

55. —— *Treasures on the Middle Way.* Berkeley: Shambhala Publications. 1976.

56. —— *The Royal Song of Saraha.* Seattle: University of Washington, 1969.

57. Hopkins, Jeffrey. *Meditation on Emptiness.* London: Wisdom Publications, 1983.

58. —— (trans. and ed.). *Meditations of a Tibetan Tantric Abbot: Kensur Lekden.* Dharamsala: LTWA, 1974.

59. —— (trans.). *Analysis of Going and Coming: The Second Chapter of Chandrakirti's "Clear Words," a Commentary on Nagarjuna's "Treatise on the Middle Way."* Dharamsala: LTWA, 1976.

60. Inada, K.K. *Nāgārjuna: Mūlamadhyamakārikā.* Tokyo: Hokuseido, 1970.

61. Jamyang Khyentse, Rinpoche. *The Opening of the Dharma: a Brief Explanation of the Essence of the Buddha's Many Vehicles.* (Translation prepared by the Translation Bureau of the Library of Tibetan Works and Archives.) Dharamsala: LTWA, 1976.

62. Kalu, Venerable Rinpoche. *The Kālacakra Empowerment: Taught by the Venerable Kalu Rinpoche.* (Translation by the Nalanda Translation Committee under the direction of Chögyam Trungpa, Rinpoche.) San Francisco: Kagya Dröden Kunchab, 1982.

63. —— *The Crystal Mirror: Clearly Showing All the Steps by Which the Path of Liberation is Traversed in This Fortunate Kalpa.* New York: Kagyu Thubten Choling, 1982.

64. —— *The Foundations of Buddhist Meditation* (trans. Ken McLeod and Kungo Lhalungpa). Vancouver, 1972; rpt. Dharamsala, LTWA, 1974.

65. K'am–trul Rinpoche, Gar-je.
"A Geography and History of Shambala" (trans. Sherpa Tulku and Alexander Berzin). In *The Tibet Journal*. Vol. 3, No. 3. Dharamsala: LTWA, 1978.

66. Kelsang Gyatso, Geshe.
Clear Light of Bliss: Mahamudra in Vajrayana Buddhism (trans. Tenzin Norbu; ed. Jonathan Landaw). London: Wisdom Publications, 1982.

67. ——
Meaningful to Behold: View, Meditation and Action in Mahayana Buddhism. An Oral Commentary to Shantideva's "A Guide to the Bodhisattva's Way of Life" (trans. Tenzin Norbu; ed. Jonathan Landaw). Cumbria: Wisdom Publications, 1980.

68. Khetsun Sangpo, Rinbochay.
Tantric Practice in Nying-ma (trans. and ed. Jeffrey Hopkins). London: Rider and Company, 1982.

69. Kongtrul, Jamgon.
The Torch of Certainty (trans. Judith Hanson). Boulder and London: Shambhala Publications, 1977.

70. Kong-sPrul the Great, 'Jam-mGon.
A Direct Path to Enlightenment: Being a Commentary Which Will Comfortably Introduce Ordinary People to "The Seven Points of Mind Training" by Atisha ([trans. Ken McLeod]. 1974; 2nd ed. Vancouver, B.C.: Kunkhyab Chuling, [1975?].

71. King, Winston L.
A Thousand Lives Away: Buddhism in Contemporary Burma. Cambridge, Massachusetts: Harvad University Press, 1964.

72. La Vallée Poussin, L. (trans.).
L'Abhidharmakośa de Vasubandhu. 6 vols. Paris: Geuthner, 1923–1931.

73. Lati Rinbochay and Jeffrey Hopkins (trans.).
Death, Intermediate State and Rebirth in Tibetan Buddhism. London, 1979; Valois, N. Y.: Gabriel Press, 1979 (?).

74.——.
Mind in Tibetan Buddhism: Oral Commentary on Geshay Jam-bel-sem-pel's "Presentation of Awareness and Know-

ledge Composite of All the Important Points. Opener of the Eye of New Intelligence" (trans. and ed. Elizabeth Napper). London, 1980; Valois, N. Y.: Gabriel Press, 1980.

75. Lessing, Ferdinand D. and Alex Wayman (trans.).
Introduction to the Buddhist Tantric Systems: Translated from Mkhas Grub Rje's Rgyud sde spyiḥi rnam par gźag pa rgyas par brjod. The Hague, 1968; 2nd ed. Delhi: Motilal Banarsidass, 1980.

76. Lévi, S. (trans.).
Mahāyāna-sutra-alamkāra de Asaṅga. 2 vols. Paris: Bibliothèque de L'École des Hautes Études, 1907.

77. Lhalungpa, Lobsang P. (trans.).
The Life of Milarepa. 2nd ed. Boulder: Prajñā Press, 1982.

78. Lobsang Tharchin, Geshe.
The Logic and Debate Tradition of India, Tibet and Mongolia. Howell, N. J.: Rashi Gempil Ling, 1979.

79. kLong-chen Rab-'byams-pa.
Kindly Bent to Ease Us: The Trilogy of Finding Comfort and Ease (trans. Herbert V. Guenther). 3 vols. Emeryville: Dharma Publishing, 1975.

80. Luk, Charles (trans. and ed.).
Vimalakīrti Niradeśa Sūtra. Berkeley and London: Shambhala, 1972.

81. Merton, Thomas.
The Wisdom of the Desert. London: Sheldon Press, 1974.

82 .———.
Zen and the Birds of Appetite. New York: New Directions Publishing Corporation, 1968.

83 Mullin, Glenn H. and Lobsang Rabgay (trans.).
Lama Mipam's Commentary to Nagarjuna's "Stanzas For a Novice Monk" together with Tsong Khapa's "Essence of the Ocean of Vinaya." Dharamsaia: LTWA, 1978.

84 Murti, T. R. V.
The Central Philosophy of Buddhism: A Study of the Mādhyamika System. 1955; 4th impression London: George Allen and Unwin, 1974.

85 Nagarjuna and Kaysang Gyatso, The Seventh Dalai Lama.
The Precious Garland and The Song of the Four Mindfulnesses (translated and edited by Jeffrey Hopkins and Lati

Rinpoche with Anne Klein). The Wisdom of Tibet Series,
2. New York: Harper and Row, 1975.
86 Nāgārjuna and Lama Mipham.
"A Letter to a Friend" [and] "The Garland of White Lotus
Flowers": A Commentary on Nāgārjuna's 'A Letter to a
Friend.' In *Golden Zephyr* (trans. Leslie Kawamura).
Emeryville: Dharma Publishing, 1975.
87 Nāgārjuna and Sakya Pandit.
"The Staff of Wisdom" by Nāgārjuna and "A Precious
Treasury of Elegant Sayings" by Sakya Pandit. In *Elegant
Sayings*. Emeryville: Dharma Publishing,1977.
88 Nagao, G. M.
A Study of Tibetan Buddhism. Tokyo: Shoten, 1954.
89. Norbu, Thubten Jigme and Colin M. Turnbull.
Tibet: Its History, Religion and People. London: Chatto
and Windus Ltd., 1969.
90A. Nyanaponika Thera.
*The Heart of Buddhist Meditation: A Handbook of Mental
Training Based on the Buddhas's Way of Mindfulness
(Satipaṭṭhāna)*. New York: Samuel Weiser, Inc., 1975.
90 B. Nyingma Institute.
Recommended Readings in Buddhist Studies. Berkeley:
Nyingmapa Institute, 1979.
91. Obermiller, E. (trans. and ed.).
History of Buddhism by Bu-ston. 2. vols. Heidelberg
1931–1932.
92. Paul, Diana Y.
*Women in Buddhism: Images of the Feminine in Mahāyāna
Tradition*. Berkeley: Lancaster-Miller Publishers, 1979.
93. Rabten, Geshe.
Echoes of Voidness (trans. Stephen Batchelor). London:
Wisdom Publications, 1983.
94. ———.
The Preliminary Practices of Tibetan Buddhism (trans.
Ven. Gonsar Tulku; comp. and ed. George Driessens).
Burton, Wash: Tusum Ling Publications, 1974.
95A. ———.
The Mind and Its Functions (trans. Stephen Batchelor).
Mt. Pèlerin: Tharpa Choeling, 1978.

95B. ———.
Levels of Consciousness: Dreaming, Death, Rebirth and Meditation. (Translated orally by the Ven. Gonsar Tulku.) Le Mont-Pèlerin: Tharpa Choeling, 1978(?).

96. Rabten, Geshe and Geshe Ngawang Dhargyey.
"Advice from A Spiritual Friend" and "Buddhist Thought Transformation": Transmitted by the Tibetan Lamas Geshe Rabten and Geshe Ngawang Dhargyey (ed. Brian Beresford, translated with Gonsar Tulku and Sherpa Tulku). Delhi: Publications for Wisdom Culture, 1977.

97. Rahula, Walopa.
What the Buddha Taught: Revised and Expanded Edition with Texts from Suttas and Dhammapada. 1959; 2nd ed. New York: Grove Press, Ic., 1974.

98. Robinson, R. H. and W. L. Johnson
The Buddhist Religion: A Historical Introduction. 2nd ed. Belmont, CA: Dickenson Publishing Company, Inc., 1977.

99. Roerich, George N. (trans.)
The Blue Annals of Gzhon-nu-dpal. 2 vols. Calcutta: Royal Asiatic Society, 1949–1953.

100. Ruegg, David S.
The Life of Bu ston Rin po che: with the Tibetan Text of the Bu ston rNam thar. Serie Orientale Roma XXXIV. Roma: Istituto Italiano per il Medio ed Estremo Oriente, 1966.

101. ———
The Literature of the Madhyamaka School of Philosophy in India. History of Indian Literature Vol. VII., Fasc. 1. Wiesbaden: Otto Harrassowitz, 1981.

102. ——— (trans.).
Le Traité du Tathāgatagarbha de Bu.ston.Rin.chen.grub: Traduction du "De bžin gšegs pa'i sñin po gsal, žin mdzes par byed pa'i rgyan." Française D'Extrême-Orient, 1973.

103. ———.
The Study of Indian and Tibetan Thought: Some Problems and Perspectives. Inaugural lecture delivered on his entrance into office as professor of Indian Philosophy, Buddhist Studies and Tibetan at the University of Leiden. Leiden: E. J. Brill, 1967.

104. Saddhatissa, H.
    Buddhist Ethics: Essence of Buddhism. New York: George
    Braziller, 1970.
105. Sangharakshita, Bhikshu.
    A Survey of Buddhism. 2nd ed. Bangalore: The Indian
    Institute of World Culture, 1959.
106. Sherburne, Richard, S. J. (trans.).
    A Lamp for the Path and Commentary of Atīśa. London:
    George Allen and Unwin Ltd., 1983.
107. Snellgrove, David and Hugh Richardson.
    A Cultural History of Tibet. London, 1968; Boulder:
    Prajñā Press, 1980.
108. Sopa, Geshe Lhundup and Jeffrey Hopkins.
    Practice and Theory of Tibetan Buddhism. New York:
    Grove Press, 1976.
109. Sprung, Mervyn (trans.).
    *Lucid Exposition of the Middle Way: The Essential
    Chapters from the "Prasannapadā" of Chandrakīrti.* Boul-
    der: Prajñā Press, 1979.
110. Stein, R. A.
    Tibetan Civilization (trans. J. E. Stapleton Driver). Lon-
    don, 1972; Standford: Standford University Press, 1972.
111. Stcherbatsky, F. T.
    Buddhist Logic. Leningrad, circa 1930; New York: Dover
    Publications, Inc., 1962.
112.—— (trans.).
    *Madhyānta-vibhaṅga: Discourse on Discrimination Be-
    tween Middle and Extremes Ascribed to Bodhisattva
    Maitreya Commented by Vasubandhu and Sthiramati.*
    Soviet Indology Series No. 5. Calcutta: Indian Studies-Past
    and present, 1971.
113. ——
    *The Central Conception of Buddhism and the Meaning of
    the Word "Dharma."* London, 1923; rpt. Delhi: Motilal
    Banarsidass, 1974.
114. ——
    The Conception of Buddhist Nirvāṇa. 1927; rpt. The
    Hague: Mouton, 1965.

115. Streng, Frederick J.
Emptiness: A Study in Religious Meaning: A Depth Study of the Philosopher Nāgārjuna and His Interpretation of Ultimate Realtity. Including Translations of Nāgārjuna's "Fundamentals of the Middle Way" and "Averting the Arguments." Nashville: Abingdon, 1967.
116. Suzuki, Daisetz T.
The Training of the Zen Buddhist Monk. Berkeley: Wingbow press, 1974.
117. ——.
Mysticism Christian and Buddhist: The Eastern and Western Way. New York: Collier Books, 1962.
118. —— (trans.).
The Lankavatara Sutra. London: Routledge and Kegan Paul, 1932.
119. ——.
Manual of Zen Buddhism. New York: Grove Press, 1978.
120. Suzuki, Ṣhunryu.
Zen Mind, Beginner's Mind. 1970; 16th printing New York and Tokyo: John Weatherhill, Inc., 1982.
121. Swearer, Donald K. (ed.).
Secrets of the Lotus: Studies in Buddhist Meditation. 1971; New York: The MacMillan Company, 1973.
122. Takasaki, Jikido.
A Study on the Ratnagotravibhāga: (Uttaratantra) Being a Treatise on the Tathāgatagarbha Theory of Mahāyāna Buddhism. Serie Orientale Roma Vol. XXXIII. Roma: Instituto Italiano per il Medio ed Estremo Oriente, 1966.
123. Tāranātha.
History of Buddhism in India (trans. Lama Chimpa and Alaka Chattopadhyaya; ed. Debiprasad Chattopadhyaya). Atlantic Highlands, N.J.: Humanities Press, 1981.
124. Tarthang Tulku.
A Gesture of Balance. Berkeley: Dharma Publishing 1977.
125. ——.
Sacred Art of Tibet. 1972; Berkeley: Dharma Publishing, 1974.

126. Thinley, Karma.
The History of the Sixteen Karmapas of Tibet. Boulder: Prajñā Press, 1980.
127. Thogs-med bzang-po and rJe Tzong-kha-pa.
The Thirty-Seven Practices of All Buddhas' Sons (rGyal-sras lag-len so-bdun-ma). Translations prepared by Geshe Ngawang Dhargyey, Sherpa Tulku, Khamlung Tulku, Alexander Berzin and Jonathan Landaw.) Dharamsala: LTWA, 1973.
128. Thomas, Edward J.
The History of Buddhist Thought. 1933; 2nd ed. 1951; rpt. London: Routledge and Kegan Paul ltd., 1971.
129. ———.
The Life of Buddha as Legend and History. 1927; London: Routledge and Kegan Paul Ltd., 1975.
130. Thondup, Tulku.
Buddhist Civilization in Tibet. 1978; U.S.A.: Maha Siddha Nyingmapa Center, 1982.
131. Thurman, Robert A. F. (trans.)
The Holy Teachings of Vimalakīrti: A Mahāyāna Scripture. 1976; rpt. University Park and London: The Pennsylvania State University Press, 1981.
132. ——— (ed.).
The Life and Teachings of Tsong Khapa (trans. Sherpa Tulku, Khamlung Tulku et alii). Dharamsala: LTWA, 1982.
133. Trinchen, Chogyay.
The History of the Sakyapa Tradition: A Feast for the Minds of the Fortunate. (Translated from Tibetan into French by Ven. Phende Rinpoche and Jamyang Khandro; from French into English by Jennifer Stott.) Bristol: Ganesha Press, 1983.
134. Trungpa, Chögyam.
Born in Tibet. London, 1966; The Clear Light Series. Boulder: Prajñā Press, 1981.
135. ———.
Visual Dharma: The Buddhist Art of Tibet. Berkeley and London: Shambhala Publications, 1975.

177

136. ——.
Meditation in Action. The Clear Light Series. Berkeley: Shambhala Publications, 1969.

137. ——.
Cutting Through Spiritual Materialism. Boulder and London: Shambhala Publications, 1973.

138. ——.
Glimpses of Abhidharma: From a Seminar on Buddhist Psychology. Boulder: Prajña Press, 1978.

139. ——.
The Myth of Freedom and the Way of Meditation. The Clear Light Series. Berkeley and London: Shambhala Publications, 1976.

140. Tsang Nyön Heruka.
The Life of Marpa the Translator: Seeing Accomplishes All. (Translated by the Nālandā Translation Committee under the direction of Chögyam Trungpa.) Boulder: Prajñā Press, 1982.

141. Tsong-ka-pa.
Tantra in Tibet: The Great Exposition of Secret Mantra. Introduced by His Holiness Tenzin Gyatso, the Fourteenth Dalai Lama. (Translated and edited by Jeffrey Hopkins.) The Wisdom of Tibet Series, 3. London: George Allen and Unwin, 1977.

142. ——.
The Yoga of Tibet: The Great Exposition of Secret Mantra: 2 and 3. Introduced by His Holiness Tenzin Gyatso, the Fourteenth Dalai Lama. (Translated and edited by Jeffrey Hopkins.) The Wisdom of Tibet Series 4. London: George Allen and Unwin, 1981.

143. ——.
Chapter two of "Ocean of Reasoning": A commentary on Nāgārjuna's "Fundamental Treatise on the Middle Way," Proving the Emptiness of Going and Coming. (Translated by Jeffrey Hopkins in accordance with instruction from Kensur Nawang Lengden.) Dharamsala: LTWA, 1974.

144. Tsong-ka-pa and Kensur Lekden.
"Illumination of the Thought: An Extensive Explanation

of Chandrakirti's 'Supplement to the Middle Way'," and "Meditations of Tantric Abbot": In *Compassion in Buddhism* (ed. and trans. Jeffrey Hopkins). London: Rider and Co., 1980.

145. Tucci, Giuseppe.
Tibetan Painted Scrolls. 2 vols. Rome, 1949; reproduced facsimile edition in 2 vols. Kyoto: Rinsen Book Co., Ltd., 1980.

146. ———.
Religions of Tibet. (Translated from German and Italian by Geoeffrey Samuel.) Berkeley and Los Angeles: University of California Press, 1980.

147. Vostrikov, A. I.
Tibetan Historical Literature. (Translated from Russian by Harish Chandra Gupta.) Soviet Indology Series No.4. Calcutta: Indian Studies – Past and Present, 1970.

148. Wallace, B. Alan (trans. and ed.).
The Life and Teaching of Geshe Rabten: A Tibetan Lama's Search for Truth. London: George Allen and Unwin, 1980.

149. Wangyal, Geshe.
The Door of Liberation. New York: Maurice Girodias Associates, Inc., 1973.

150. Warren, Henry Clarke (trans.).
Buddhism in Translations: Passages Selected from the Buddhist Sacred Books and Translated from the Original Pāli into English. 1962; New York: Atheneum, 1976.

151. Wylie, Turrell V.
The Geography of Tibet According to the 'Dzamgling-rgyas-bshad. Serie Orientale Roma Vol. XXV. Roma: Istituto Italiano per il Medio ed Estremo Oriente, 1962.

152. Yeshe, Lama and Zopa Rinpoche.
Wisdom Energy: Basic Buddhist Teachings (ed. Jonathan Landaw with Alex Berzin). 1976; 2nd printing London: Wisdom Publications, 1982.

153. Zahler, Leah (ed.).
Meditative States in Tibetan Buddhism: The Concentrations and Formless Absorptions. (Lati Rinbochay's Oral Pre-

sentation translated by Jeffrey Hopkins; Pan-chen Sö-
nam-drak-ba's "Explanation of the Concentrations and
Formless Absorptions" translated by Leah Zahler; De-
nma Lochö Rinbochay's Oral Commentary translated by
Jeffrey Hopkins.) London: Wisdom Publications. 1983.